behind the canvas

40 ARTISTS WORKING IN WEST CORNWALL

sarah brittain & simon cook

TRURAN

For Dom

Thanks to Blair Todd, Sue Sharrocks, Lou Brittain, Michael & Hayley Jay, Heather & Ivan Corbett

Special thanks to all of the artists for their time, enthusiasm and hospitality

To Dan, Sam, Jess and Billy

Published by Truran, Croft Prince, Mount Hawke, Truro, Cornwall TR4 8EE
www.truranbooks.co.uk

ISBN 1 85022 159 6 (paperback)
ISBN 1 85022 160 X (cased)

Printed and bound in Cornwall by R. Booth (Bookbinders) Ltd & Troutbeck Press, Antron Hill, Mabe, Penryn, Cornwall TR10 9HH

THE ARTISTS

Wilhelmina Barns-Graham
Noel Betowski
Sandra Blow
Bob Bourne
Neil Canning
Richard Cook
Jessica Cooper
Michael Finn
Naomi Frears
Ralph Freeman
Anthony Frost
Sir Terry Frost
Rose Hilton
Sax Impey
Kurt Jackson
Graham Jobbins
Robert Jones
Rachael Kantaris
David Kemp
Jeremy Le Grice
Alexander Mackenzie
Daphne McClure
Margo Maeckelberghe
Maggie Matthews
June Miles
John Miller
Paul Mount
Anton Nickson
Breon O'Casey
Biddy Picard
Neil Pinkett
Simon Pooley
Roy Ray
Tom Rickman
Alex Smirnoff
Mary Stork
Maurice Sumray
Michael Upton
Gill Watkiss
Partou Zia

SARAH BRITTAIN

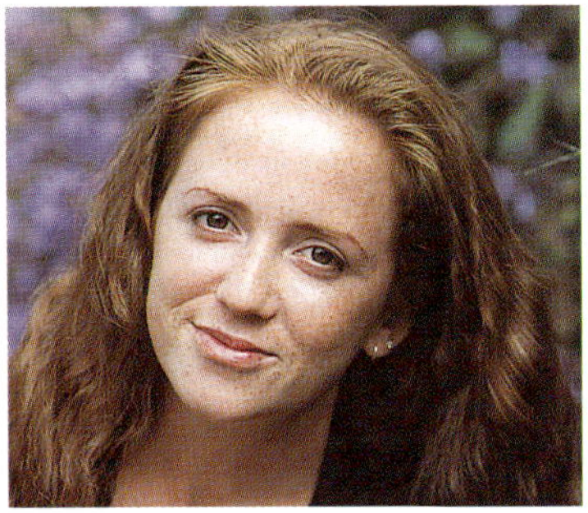

Sarah Brittain was born in 1975 and at a young age moved to St Just, Penwith where she now lives with her husband Dom. She graduated in Illustration from Falmouth College of Art in 1996 and has since illustrated children's books for international clients through her agents in London and New York. In 1997 she was involved in the international arts event 'The Quality of Light' and in the same year became manager of the Great Atlantic Mapworks Gallery in St Just.

She has taught art part-time at Cape Cornwall School and as a result of working on a specific art project with pupils, the school won the prestigious 'Artworks, National Children's Art Awards, 2001' with the awards ceremony at the Tate Modern.

SIMON COOK

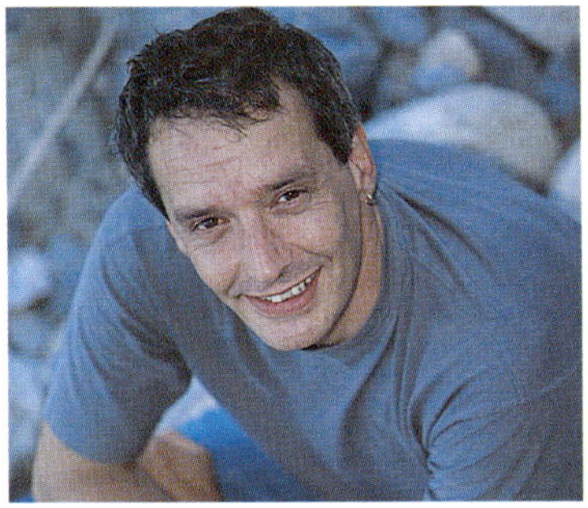

(Steve Tanner)

Simon Cook was born in 1960 at Ding Dong in Penwith, Cornwall, leaving the county in the early 80s for London. He returned twelve years later having trained and worked in the city as a commercial photographer.

Back in Cornwall he soon gained recognition for his weekly 'Penwith Landscape' feature in *The Cornishman* and in the mid 90s started to specialise in the photography of fine art for local artists and craftspeople. Today his pictures appear in numerous publications, both national and local. He is the principal photographer for the National Trust in Cornwall and produces work for subjects as diverse as scientific instrument manufacturers and local government.

INTRODUCTION

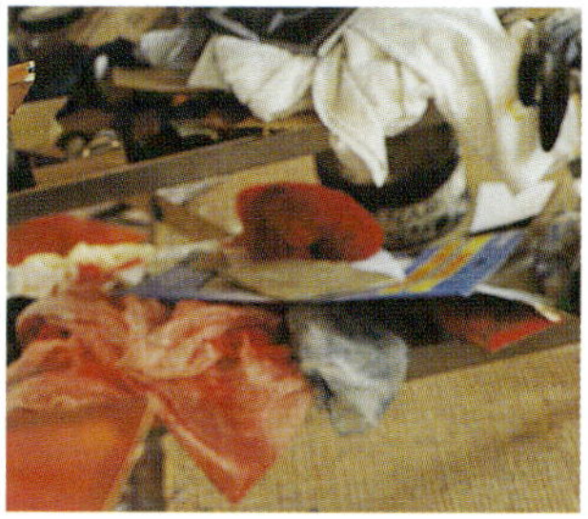

Behind the Canvas is an exploration into the lives of forty artists living and working in Penwith in the far west of Cornwall.

Penwith has long been recognised as significant in the art world from the formation of the Newlyn School of Painters in the late 19th century to the post-war modernists of St Ives. More recently the artistic community has continued to grow from these foundations and thrive, being a home and workplace to many artists throughout this western peninsula.

Penwith now boasts both established artists who have an international reputation and also new artists who are receiving recognition in Cornwall and elsewhere in the country. Many of us can identify the paintings or sculpture of this region's best-known artists, but know little or nothing of the individual behind the work. It is these artists, both long established and those younger faces whose studios I visited, whether perched on the edge of the wild Botallack cliffs or hidden above a hairdressers in Penzance who form the contents of this book. Hundreds of talented and successful artists live in Penwith, making the task of limiting those chosen to forty, a difficult one. Those represented here show the diversity of painters, sculptors and printmakers across the region.

I feel fortunate to have grown up amongst the moorland and stone circles that surround St Just and find it unsurprising that so many have been drawn to this western tip of Britain as it seems to epitomise everything that Cornwall is loved for: dramatic cliffs, rocky granite outcrops, bleak moors strewn with purple and yellow heather and gorse, busy fishing ports and a

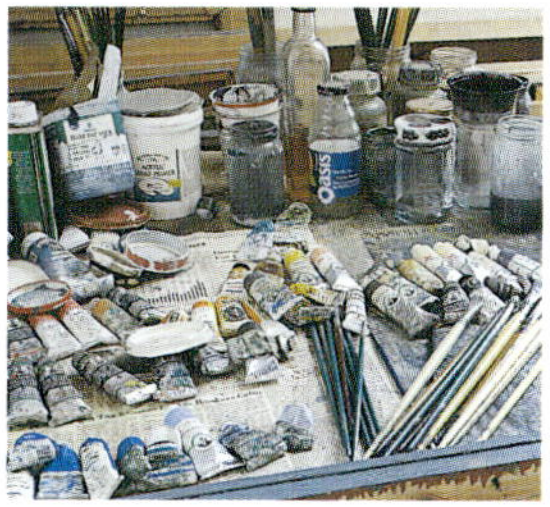

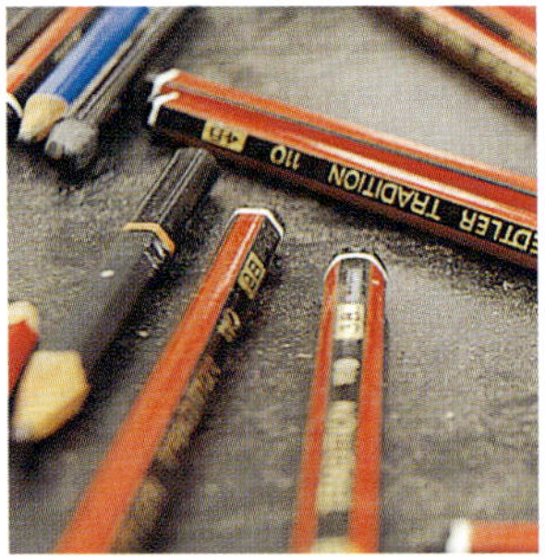

landscape littered with the ruins of a tin mining industry. It is a place of extremes, in summer you can take your pick of beautiful beaches with sunlight glinting off the Atlantic and in winter the mist, wind and rain seem all-pervading. All artists, no matter what their medium are inspired by their surroundings and this combined with the opportunity to work alongside like-minded creative people has made Penwith an irresistible home.

As the manager of a local art gallery, The Great Atlantic Mapworks, I am lucky enough to visit many artists and see the work in the context of their own studios. Local photographer Simon Cook also works with many artists in the area so it was therefore an obvious choice for us to collaborate on this project. One of my main roles in the gallery is to provide an insight to the personalities behind the work for visitors: 'Has she always lived in Cornwall?' 'Where does he get his inspiration from?' There is a fascination for the people who make the work, a human, personal interest in who they are. To satisfy their curiosity and my own, it is those questions that I put to the artists featured in this book. Interviews ranged from a fifteen-minute question and answer session to hours spent chatting, sipping wine and nibbling cheese with the forgotten questions pushed under a chair. I always returned with so much that was exciting, interesting and relevant that it became difficult to condense them.

The interviews represent the artists in their own words rather than serious art criticism and although different questions were asked of each artist, there were some recurring similarities. Artists working in this area feel fortunate to be doing so. Some are native to Cornwall but most have been drawn to the

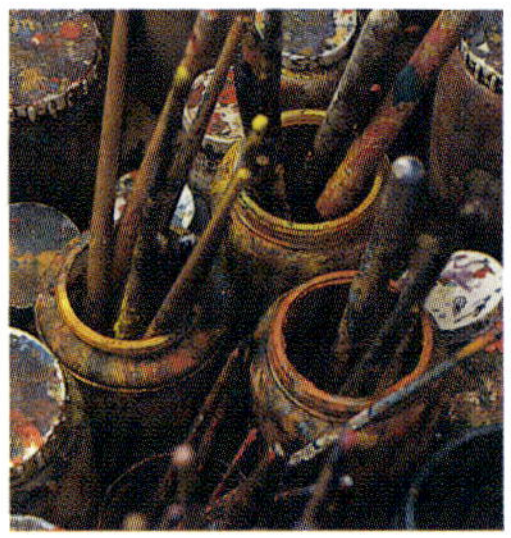

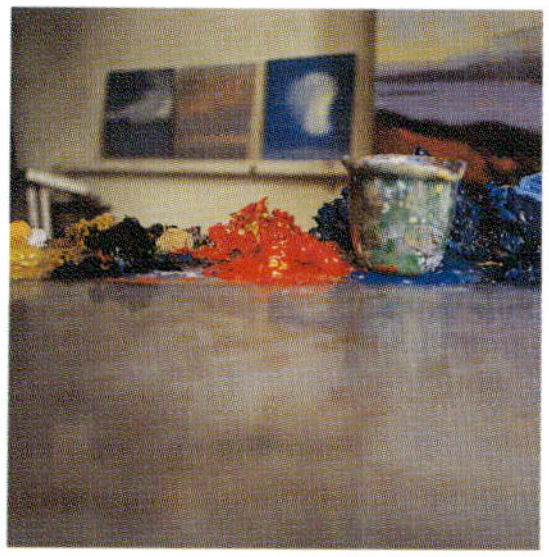

history, the chance to be a part of a supportive artistic community and also the land itself. The wildness and remoteness of Penwith has an unmistakable influence on the work and many agree that were they to live in another area, then what they produce would be remarkably different. However remote their surroundings may sometimes seem, the knowledge that there is another artist around the corner, struggling with and rejoicing in what they too have chosen for their life, is of huge support and significance. It is not a job, it's a way of life and one of the intrinsic parts of producing the work appears to be sharing it: to have a visual conversation. Whether the viewer dislikes the work or falls in love with it, a connection is made and the artist is not working alone. Most refuse to look upon their work as a career, instead focusing their ambitions on producing work they can be proud of.

I have discovered that the varied artists portrayed in this book are honest, genuine and engaging personalities who are just as exciting as the work they produce. I hope that these interviews combined with Simon Cook's wonderful portrait photography bring greater understanding as well as a glance into the lives of those artists behind the canvas.

Sarah Brittain

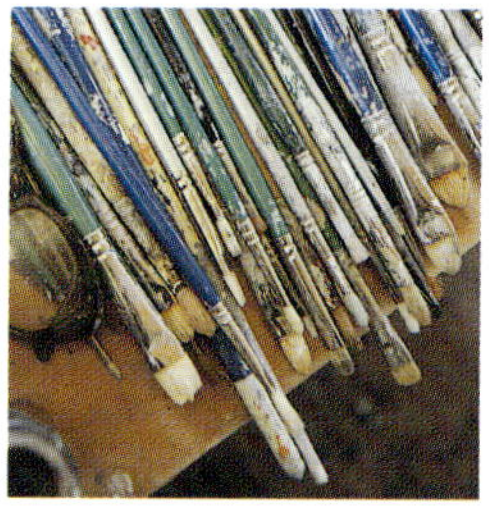

WILHELMINA BARNS-GRAHAM
CBE HRSA HSWA D.Litt. D.Art

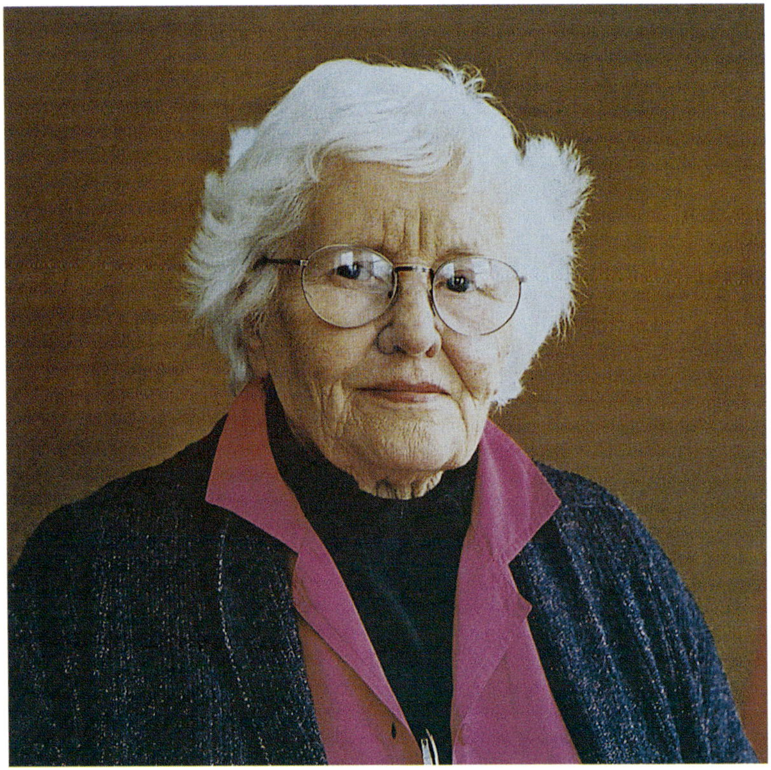

Wilhelmina Barns-Graham was born in St Andrews in 1912 and studied at Edinburgh College of Art, graduating DAE in 1936. She received a postgraduate travelling award in 1937. Moving to St Ives in 1940, she became a founder member of the Penwith Society of Arts and met Borlase Smart, Leonard Fuller, Ben Nicholson, Barbara Hepworth, Naum and Miriam Gabo, Bernard Leach, John Wells, Denis Mitchell and Sven Berlin. From the 1930s to 1950s she visited Paris, Italy and Spain, winning the Italian Government travelling award in 1955. After visiting America in 1967, she visited Barcelona and worked in Lanzarote during the 1980s and 1990s. The exhibition 'An Enduring Image' was held at the Tate, St Ives in 1999-2000.

bruary 2000
0 x 770mm
rylic on arches paper
avid Roche)

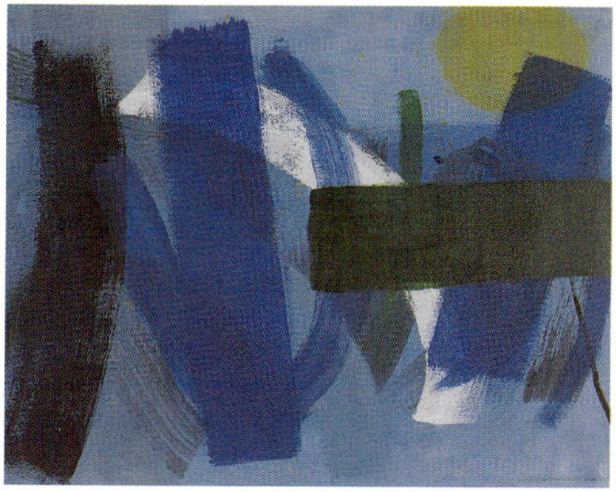

I was eight years old when I knew I wanted to be an artist. In my teens I discovered Cezanne. I have always been interested in drawing. The discovery of abstract shapes, the effect of the sun on glaciers, rain on clay country, wind on sand, the volcanic rocks of Sicily and Lanzarote. After sessions of drawing I turn my back on the experience and return to painting in the abstract where there is a meeting point of abstracted ideas. This swing of outward observation and inward perception or vice versa, has always increased my awareness. I tend to work in themes, some of these lasting years. During the late 1940s - 1950s I experimented with the Golden Section. In the early 1950s I restricted my palette to earth colours, expanding into more primary colours by the 1960s, after a visit to Spain in 1958, making a colour note sing in space. 1959 studying philosophic and theological ideas, I became involved with relationships, 'Things of a kind in Order and Disorder'.

I have an urgency and purpose to paint the celebration of life. The positive aspect of working in the abstract is the freedom of choice in medium and texture, only using that which perfects or adds to the idea, sometimes taking risks. The importance of colour, structure and space, enjoying the colour until that moment of excitement, the held breath - when the work tells me what to do and appears to speak and sing.

NOEL BETOWSKI

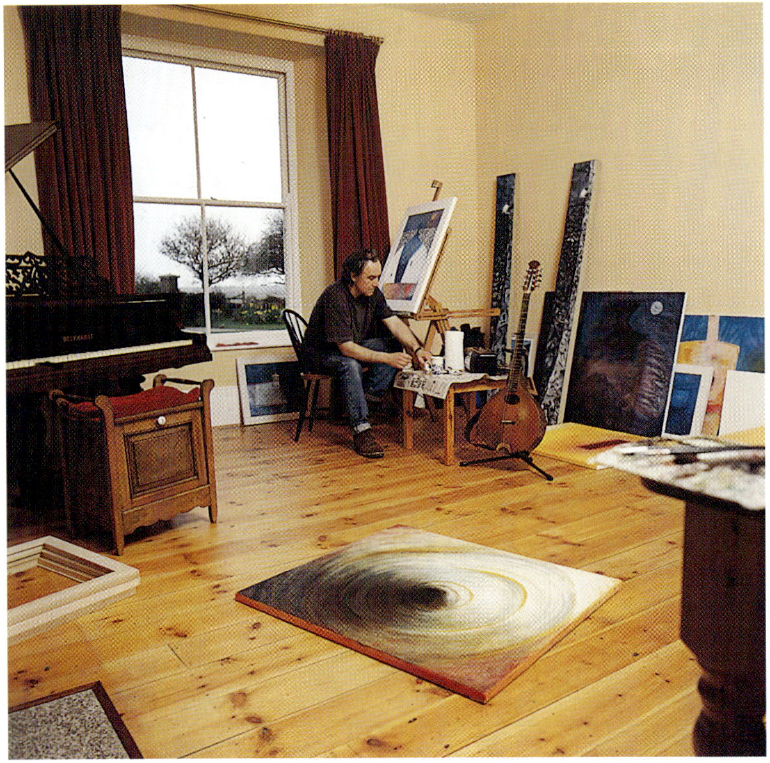

Painter and musician Noel Betowski was born in Essex in 1952. He studied at the Central School of Art and London University, Institute of Education. He lives in Sancreed where he paints, composes and plays music with his wife Pam.

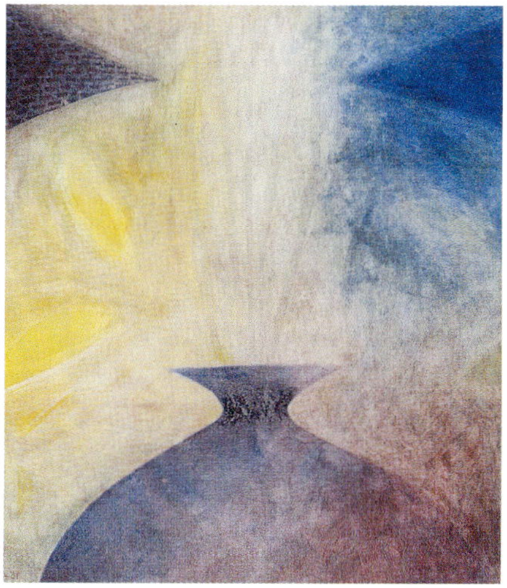

Vessel
2000
915 x 760mm
oil on canvas

When I moved to Cornwall with Pam and my son Paul in 1987 my paintings changed enormously. In London I had worked on large representational paintings, based on the drawings that often took weeks to complete while visiting Cornwall. After moving here I envisaged using the same style and subject matter as before, representing crumbling and decaying buildings, but I probably had a very romantic image about the area and gradually that romance evaporated. What inspired me about Cornwall was the feeling of remoteness, mystery and the barren landscape around St Just, but for some reason I no longer wanted to paint this subject matter and my work changed direction. From an upstairs window I glimpsed the sea beyond the gable end of a house and a rooftop. I started a series of very simplified drawings that eventually led to paintings, minimalist compared to earlier work, and I am still developing concepts in my paintings from that period.

I consider my paintings and music as being part of the same creative process. While painting I feel within a constant rhythm, pulse or beat and in many paintings I try to express this 'rhythmic flow' as abstract wave patterns or the current of water in the sea. When recording our own musical compositions, which I prefer to call 'sound sculptures' in the studio, it relates directly to the process of painting - creating layers of textures in sound. My work is, I hope, a method of communication; it is a language where I endeavour to speak to all cultures.

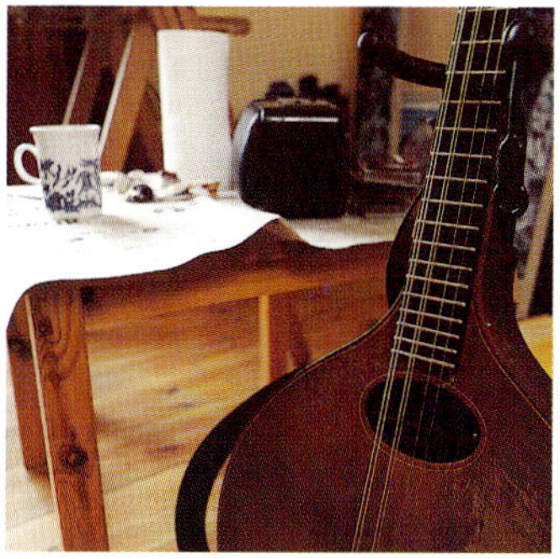

SANDRA BLOW

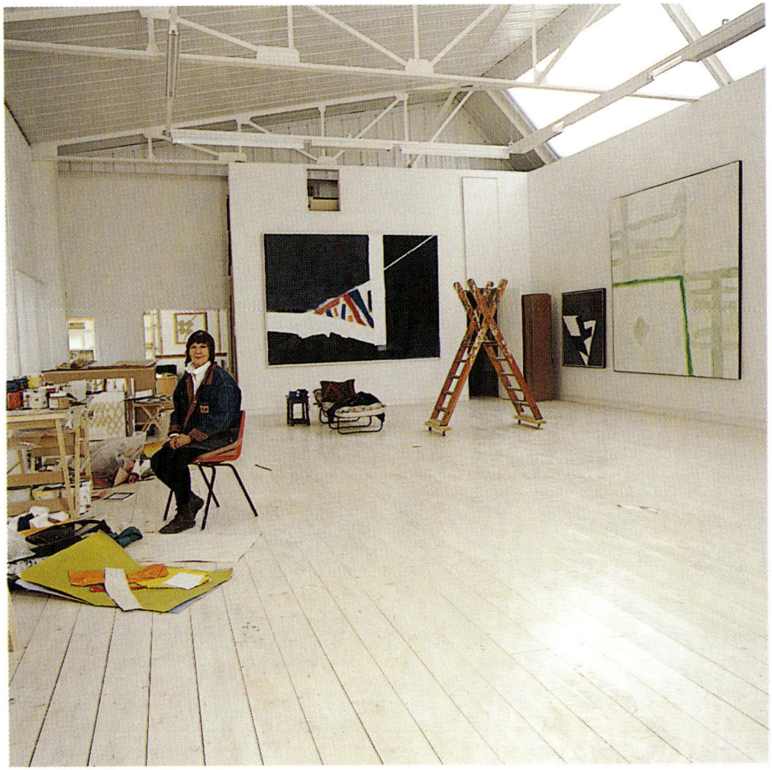

Born in London in 1925, Sandra Blow studied at St Martin's College of Art and the Royal Academy. She lived in Italy for a year in the late 1940s and then spent a year travelling in Spain and France. She returned to London in 1950 and began teaching at the Royal College in 1960. She moved to St Ives in 1994.

Untitled
2001
465 x 465mm
acrylic/paper
collage

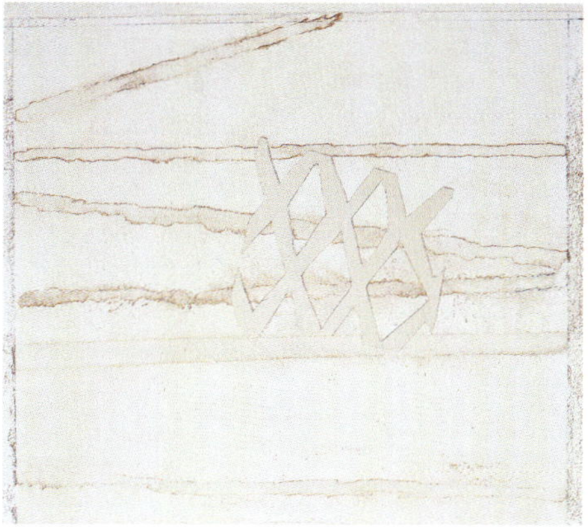

I came to Penwith on holiday with Roger Hilton in 1957 and stayed with Patrick Heron for a week and decided to take a small cottage at Zennor for a year so I could see all four seasons. I had always been interested in landscapes and I think a certain landscape quality then entered my work. It was a wonderful and very sociable time and there was a lot of dancing and partying and I became friends with many artists such as Bryan Wynter and Peter Lanyon. However, I'm a Londoner by birth and at that time it was essential to be in the capital for many reasons and so at the end of the year I decided to return. The reason for finally settling in Cornwall was that over the years, the rent on my beloved studio in London, which I'd had since 1960, rose from £3 to £300 a week and would continue to rise and in the end I would just be working to pay the landlord.

I usually work within a certain range of ideas and I've noticed that the paintings I do are very connected, they grow out of each other, when I'm working on one I can see possibilities of another and it leads on and often themes get repeated. I find at the age I am now, that the effort needed for the very large paintings is a bit much and I'm more comfortable working on a smaller size. I still paint every day, even at weekends. It's my way of life.

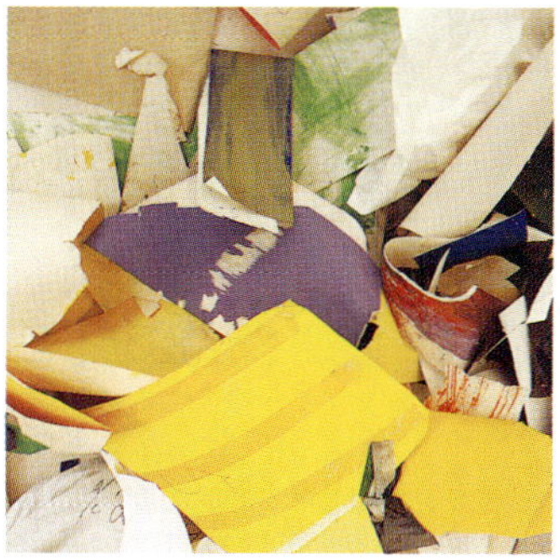

BOB BOURNE

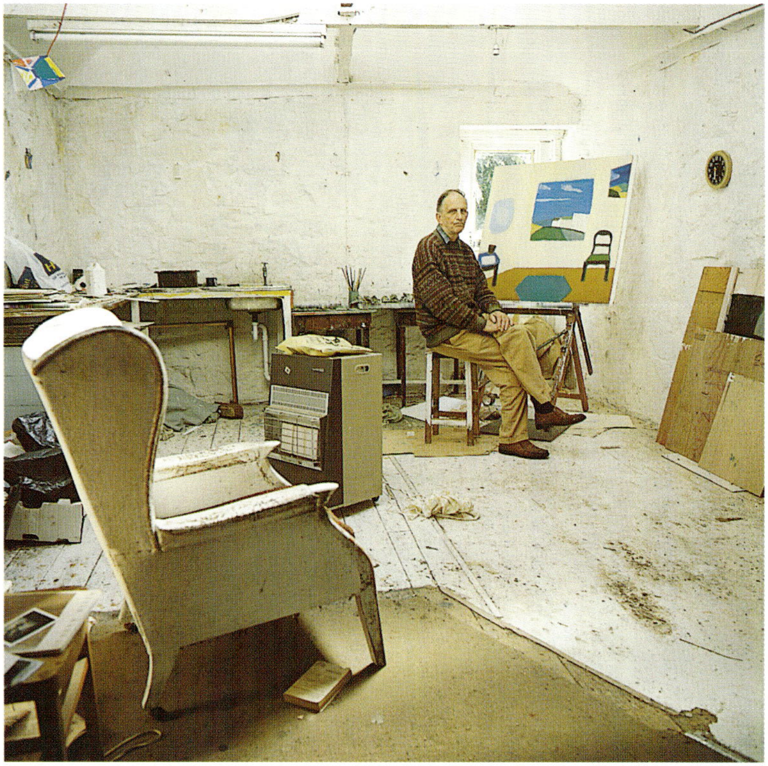

The self-taught painter Bob Bourne was born in 1931 and brought up in Exmouth, Devon. He moved to Cornwall in 1960 and spent a couple of years in Australia in the 1970s. He lives and works in Penzance.

Blue Skies
2000
860 x 860mm
oil on plywood

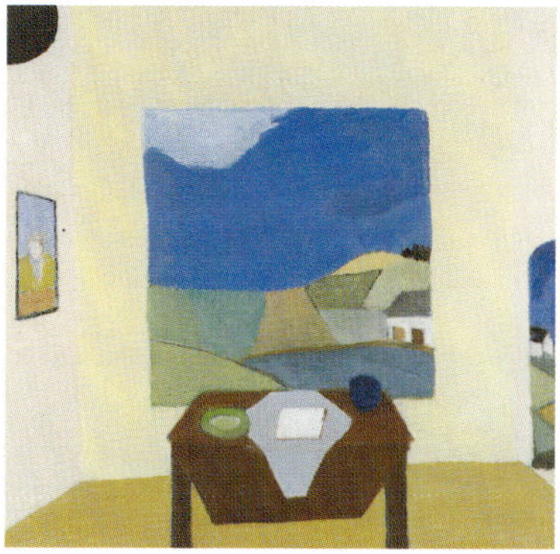

I was given a set of paints for Christmas in 1950 and my interest in painting gradually developed from there. I've had no official training and I regret not going to art college, because if I had I would have been on the conveyor belt of contacts. But I'm sure it would have changed my work, I might not be painting at all now if I had gone because it can stifle you. When I came to Cornwall there were a lot of good artists here like Lanyon and Hilton and I learnt more from them than I ever would have at art school just by watching them and talking to them. In those days people were open, you would visit each other's studios, talk in the pub; it was a totally different world. In the late 60s and early 70s the art world changed so much, it became so competitive. Artists learnt how to market themselves and the work became commercialised.

My paintings start from a square on the canvas and evolve and balance in an abstract way. I was tremendously influenced by the way Roger Hilton used his canvas. My vision has always been representational but at times it comes close to abstraction. My paintings in a way are always open, they set a scene which allows the viewer to make up their own assumptions from looking at them. Painting is the only thing I can do well and if a painting works it gives me a tremendous lift both spiritually and physically. You can make it what you want.

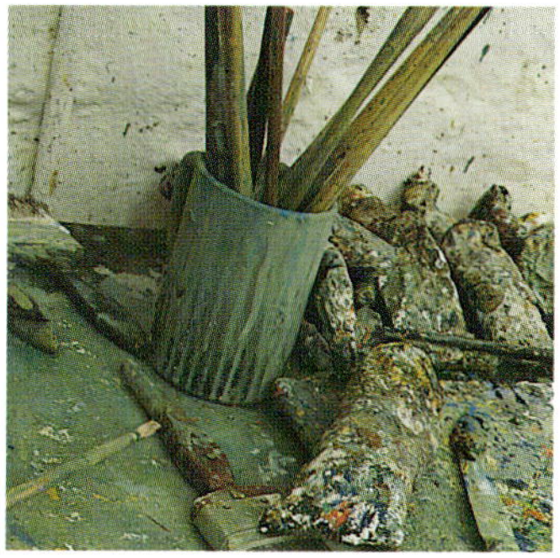

NEIL CANNING

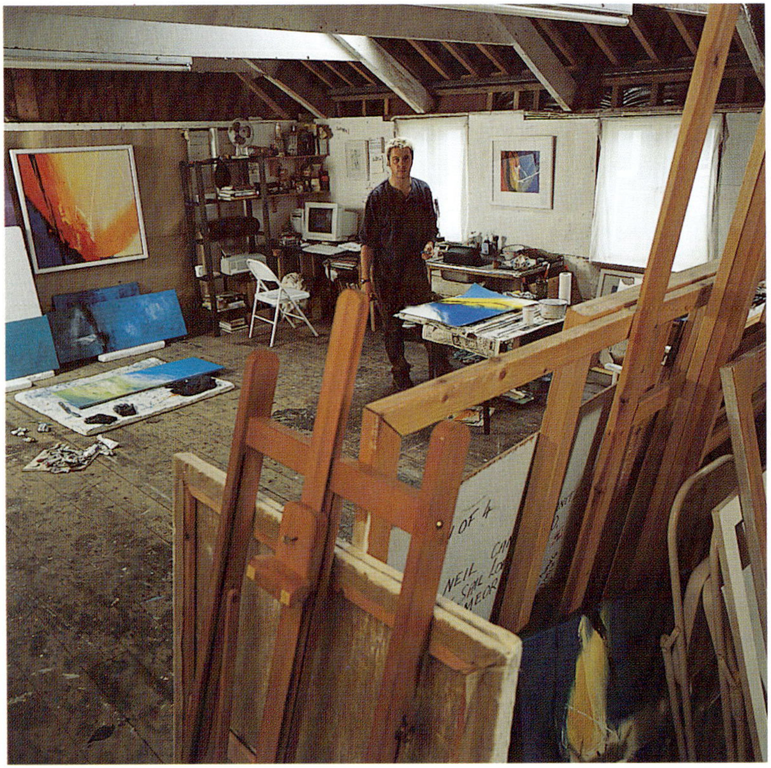

Neil Canning was born in Oxfordshire in 1960. Over the last twenty years his reputation has been steadily growing and his work has been purchased by collectors worldwide. He is also represented in many major corporate collections including ICI, Rolls Royce and Nat West Bank. He lives in Hayle and works from a studio in St Ives.

Sanctuary
2000
910 x 910mm
oil on canvas

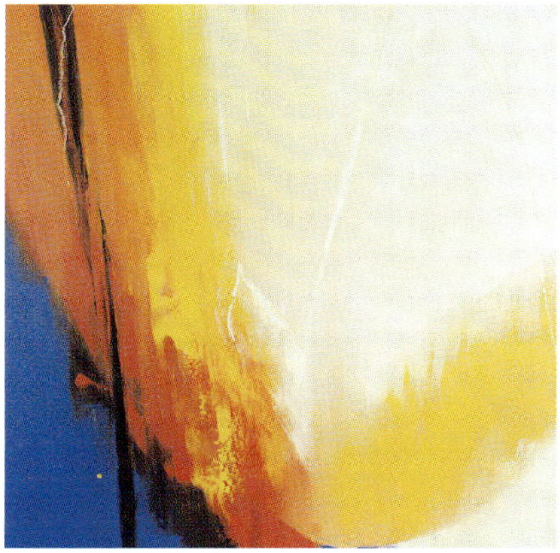

Since moving to West Penwith four years ago my work has changed quite drastically. After working in the soft, river valleys of Oxfordshire and then the protecting hills of Wales, Cornwall had a dramatic impact. It was very liberating to be suddenly right on the edge of the land, surrounded by ocean. To sit on a cliff top and be aware of the curve of the earth is an amazing experience: it made me aware of the curve of time and space in a very poignant way. This environment is obviously visually stimulating but it has also encouraged me to approach the way I paint with a more open mind.

The main thread of my work has always revolved around my response to landscape. As my painting has progressed over the last twenty years I have become more aware that it is not enough for me just to record a topographical scene. What I now wish to convey is my emotional response to nature. After spending time exploring a particular location I make a few very simple drawings and some written notes, these are just used to bring me back to the original experience once I am in the studio. Memory plays an important role in the way this information is distilled and for this reason I choose not to work directly in front of my subject. More recently my work has become much more abstracted and pure colour now plays an increasingly vital role.

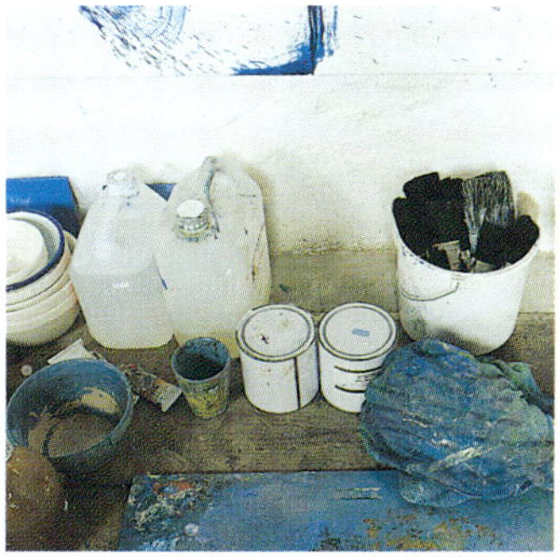

RICHARD COOK

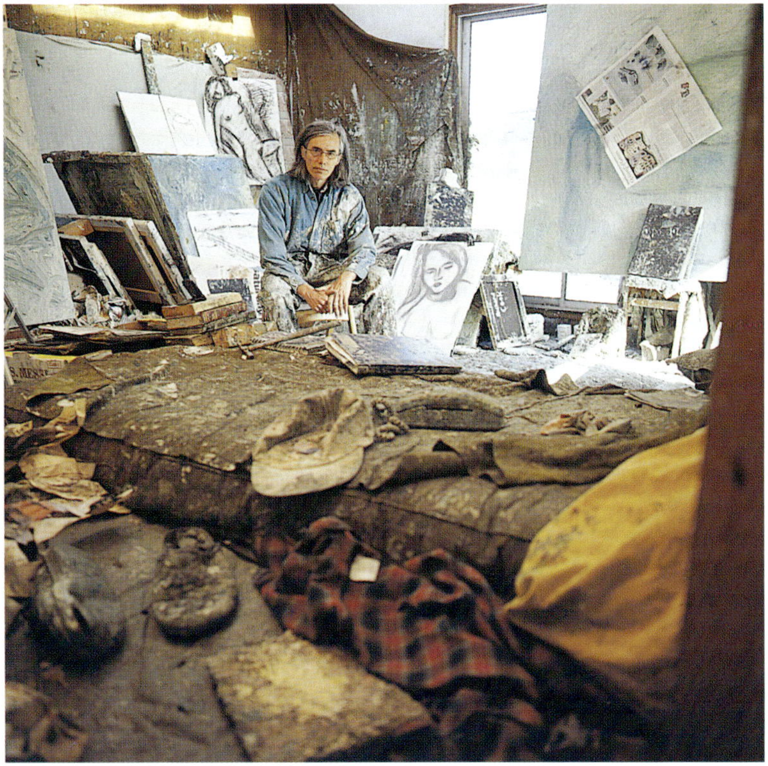

Richard Cook was born in Cheltenham in 1947 and spent his early childhood in Ceylon (present day Sri Lanka), returning to England in 1954. He trained at St Martin's School of Art and the Royal College of Art. He moved from London to Newlyn in 1985. His most recent exhibition was 'Luminous' at the Tate Gallery, St Ives in 2001.

May Morning, Lelant
122 x 152cm
oil on panel
(Colin Mills)

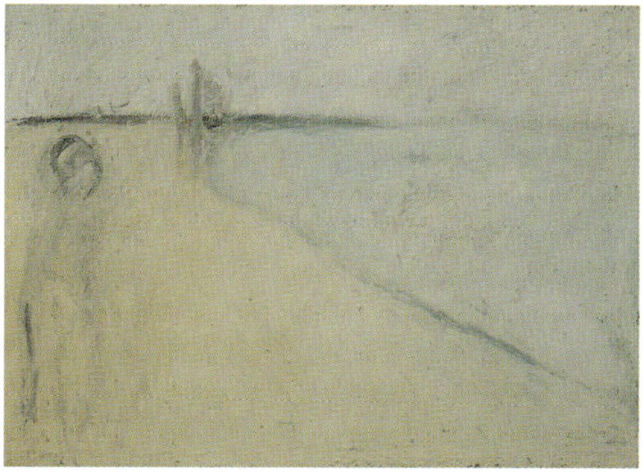

I am a painter of landscape and weather. The outdoors and places where I walk and which I know are my subject matter. For the past fifteen years, living and working in Cornwall, I have built an affinity with certain landmarks and areas. These places are not necessarily attractive because of any remarkable quality in them, it is more that I have over time, established an emotional rapport between my processes and place as subject.

These landscapes have for me transcended their everyday reality. The sense of familiarity I have built over time, has moved these apparently ordinary spots onto the realm of the nameless. However, landscape is only made accessible to me through my need to draw and paint from the human form. So in some strange way, land, sky and tree become interwoven with body, face and soul.

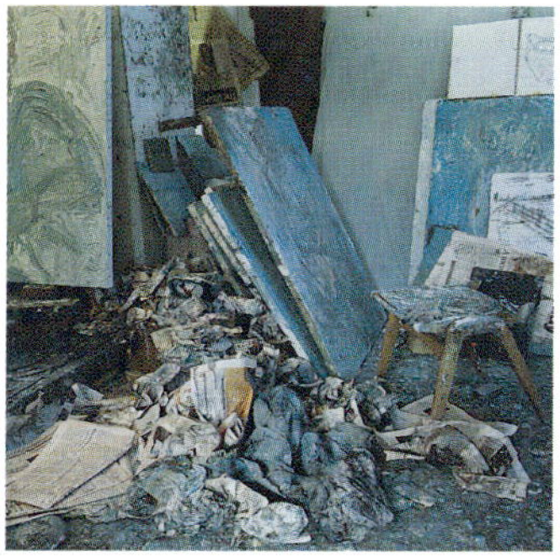

JESSICA COOPER

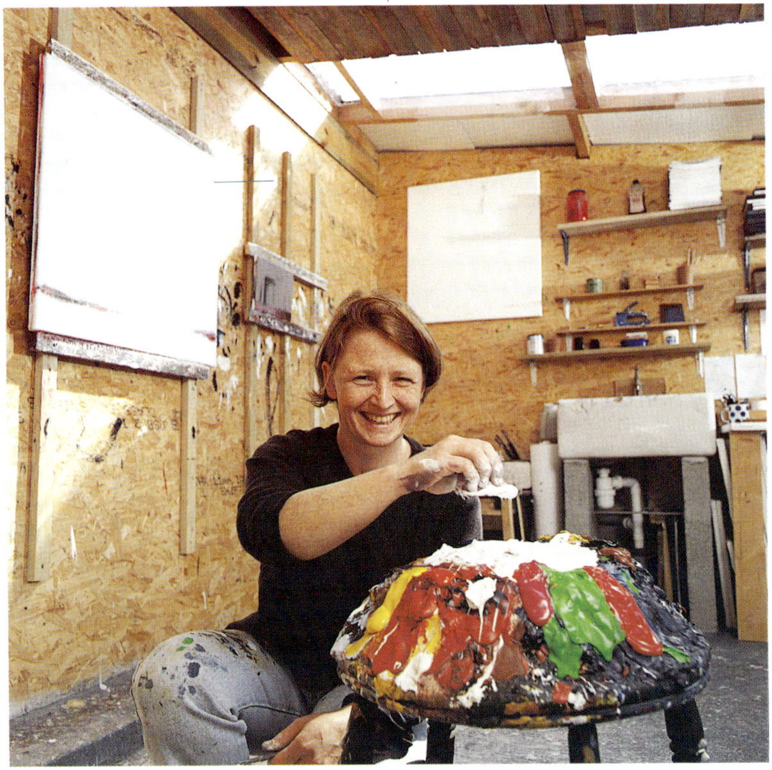

Born in Bristol in 1967, Jessica Cooper moved to West Cornwall at a young age. She studied at Falmouth College of Art and Goldsmiths College, London. She now lives in Pendeen with her husband and two children. A member of the Newlyn Society of Artists, she is also closely involved with education at both Newlyn and the Tate, St Ives.

You Can Do No Wrong
810 x 860mm
acrylic and pencil on canvas

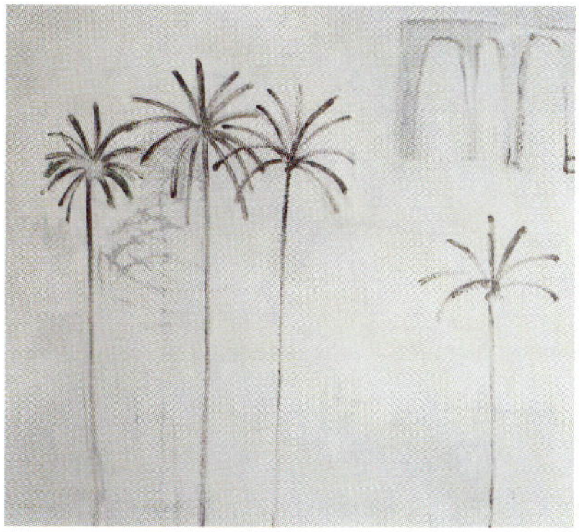

I am aware of many other artists working in West Penwith and it is not unlike being a small pea in a great bowl. But painting is part of me and has always been there. When I was four years old I wrote a card which said 'Dear Daddy, when I grow up I want to be an artist'. Painting is a constant in my life.

One of the things I really like about living in Penwith is the space. The huge expanses of sky, sea and landscape produce an intensity of feeling and influence my work more and more. I am constantly aware of my surroundings and of absorbing things that later come out in my work.

My technique is quite unusual. The paint appears to be applied very thinly but in fact is layer upon layer. When partly dry, the paint is washed off, some resists and some is removed completely, then another layer is put on. I work in two ways, swinging between being very painterly where drawing and order are almost lost and the whole canvas is enveloped in atmosphere, to my more minimal work where I'll have perhaps one colour with a drawn image which is quite structured.

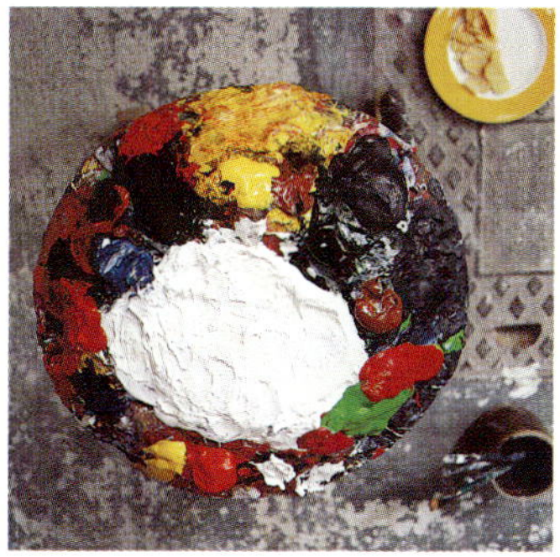

MICHAEL FINN

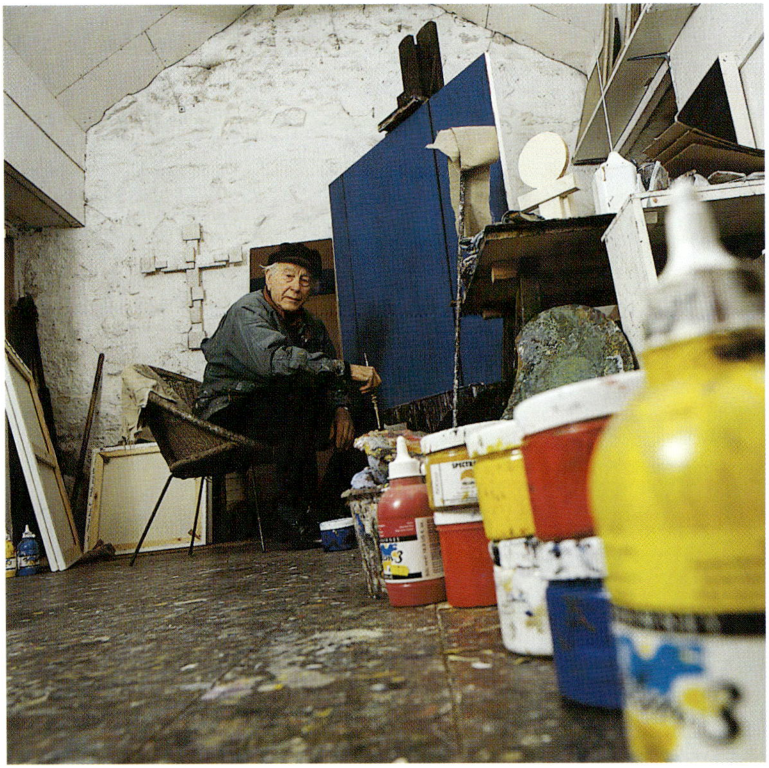

Michael Finn was born in 1921 and grew up in Surrey. He attended Kingston School of Art before joining the RAF in 1942 and training as a pilot in Canada. After the war he completed his studies at the Royal College of Art and began a teaching career, which included fourteen years as principal of Falmouth School of Art and ten years as principal of Bath Academy of Art. He retired in 1982 to paint full-time and moved to St Just.

Untitled
2000
1015 x 1015mm
acrylic on canvas

I first became interested in art when I visited the Tate Gallery as a schoolboy. I remember seeing a painting of an interior with a seated figure in front of a window, through which you could see people walking in a park. It had an incredible languor about it and the idea that a painting could be so evocative struck me as being magical. It was an experience I shall never forget and was the first time I fell in love with the idea of painting. Not surprisingly for that time I painted figuratively for many years - mostly landscapes and only occasionally making images that seemed personal. When abstraction became fashionable I thought it was not for me, although my first encounter with American colour-field painting left me very excited.

In 1971 I made an abstract construction using the backs of canvases, board, paper and wood which looked better than any of my previous figurative work, it seemed more meaningful and from that moment on I produced mostly non-figurative paintings and constructions.

I am rather in the dark about what I do except that it feels right for me and seems to be within a tradition that is nearly a century old and yet it is still possible to make something very personal, which I think is wonderful.

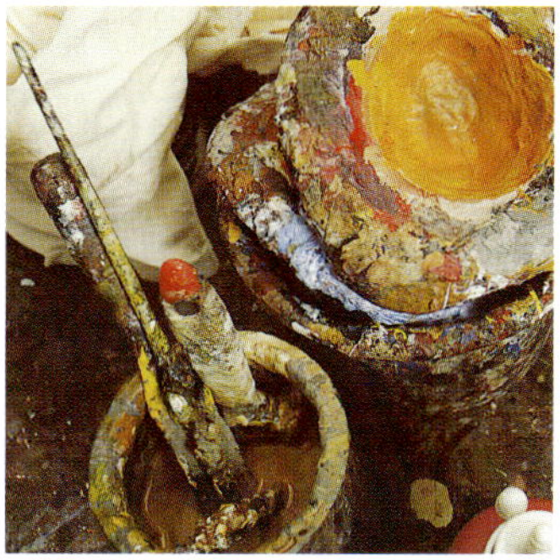

NAOMI FREARS

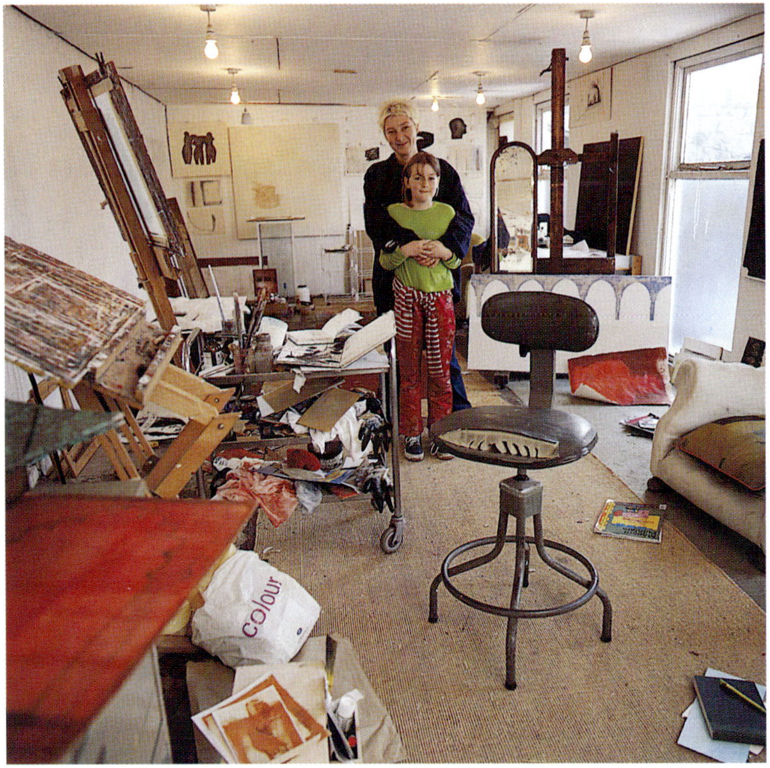

Painter and printmaker Naomi Frears was born in Leicestershire in 1963. She studied at Loughborough Art College and Sunderland College of Art. She settled in St Ives in 1989 where she lives with her husband and daughter.

Boy Next Door
1999
305 x 345mm
acrylic on canvas
(Bob Berry)

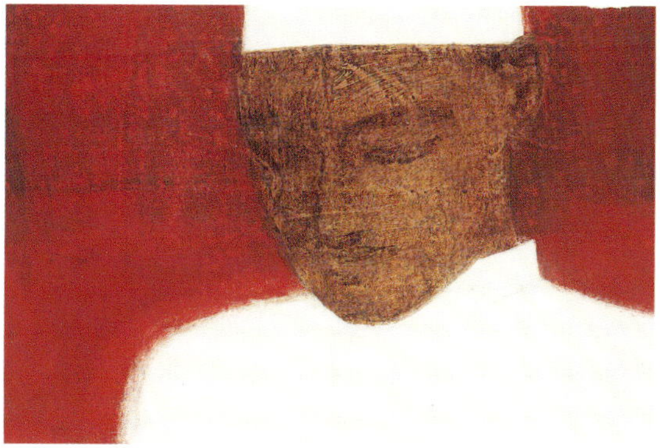

I thought I was going to be a doctor so did science at school, not art. I was just finding out that I wasn't cut out for medicine when I won a competition to spend three months in a French school. I took a sketchbook with me just in case. Back in Britain my teachers saw the drawings and put me in for the 'O' level. I didn't do the 'A' level but decided to try and go to art college because it looked like a wonderful and cushy life. It was and I made bad sculptures and was so lazy that I was chucked out for a year. I was horrified but this was the shock I needed. In my year off I spent two fantastic months at Cyprus College of Art. I switched to the print studio for my final year and won the printmaking prize.

After travelling then settling in St Ives I started making work again by joining Sheila Oliner's printmaking classes. With encouragement from Sheila and, unusually maybe, the birth of my daughter I became an enthusiastic and committed artist. I couldn't believe I'd found the thing I was meant to be doing.

In my work I tend to find images, lose them and find them again. I worry my work to death and feel desperate when I've got an exhibition deadline, as I'm quite happy to work on paintings forever. There are stages when I am seduced by a painting or despair of it but I've never ever said 'that'll do'. A painting is finished when it can stand alone without me having the urge to grab it and change it.

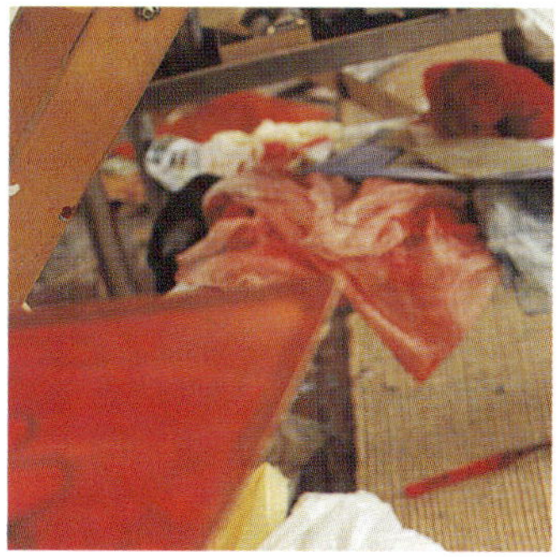

RALPH FREEMAN

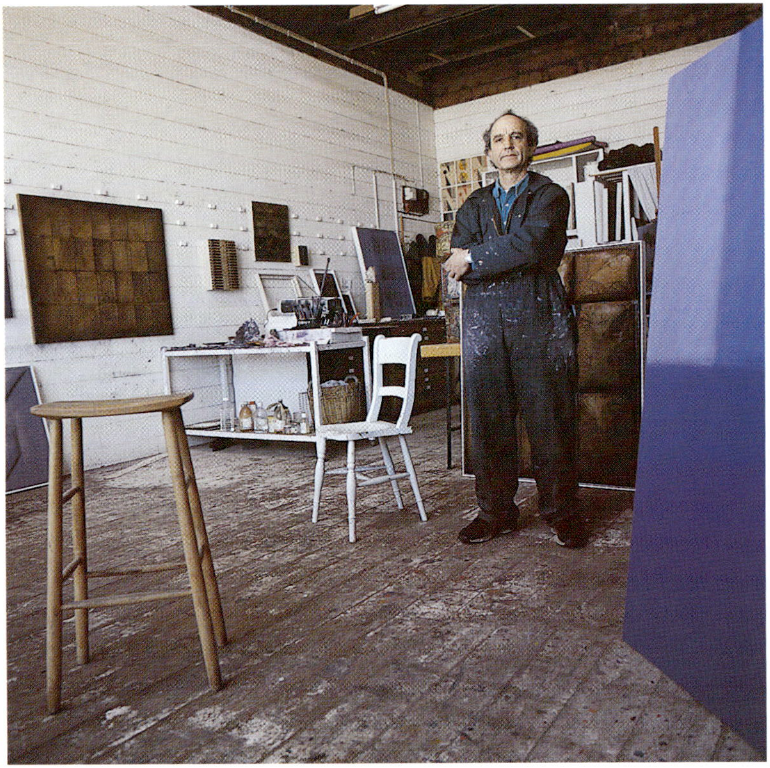

Artist and musician Ralph Freeman was born in London in 1945. He studied at St Martin's and Harrow Schools of Art and also worked as a designer, lecturer, jazz pianist and composer. As an artist he has shown widely with solo exhibitions in Britain and Continental Europe. In 1997/98, the Tate Gallery, St Ives exhibited the body of works, 'Foundations and Fragments' which subsequently toured. This represents an ongoing series of collages relating to his family and its history.

'The Letter'
2000
490 x 550mm
mixed media
relief on canvas

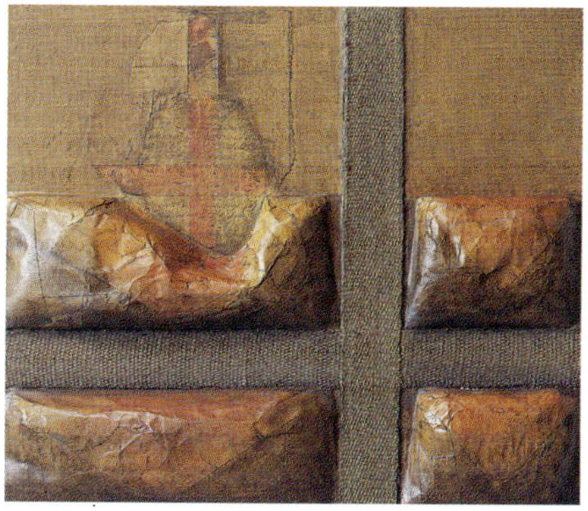

As an artist who also happens to be a musician, I couldn't do without either creative form, one informs the other. The process is similar except that music is linear - it happens over time - whereas painting is planar - it can be seen at once. Music can be more interactive and technically demanding, but the artist works alone which can be more personally demanding.

Drawing shows me what I don't want to do in a painting or construction, a kind of exorcism or shortcut. But in the end I still have to work everything out on the canvas, trying to pare down to essentials.

For many years, I worked outdoors from the landscape, eventually coming to abstraction through a natural process, because working in front of something was not quite enough, so I returned to the studio.

My work is about abstract principles: divisions of space, balance, form, tone, colour. There are so many elements in a work that can come together in mysterious ways. If we could use words to describe this process we wouldn't need art. I try to be open and let the work take me on its course. I often think it's not really up to the artist; it's the work that says what to do, where to go. The artist is just a vehicle.

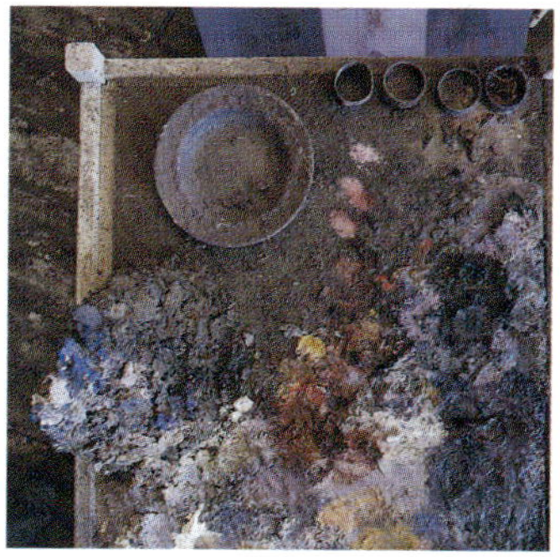

ANTHONY FROST

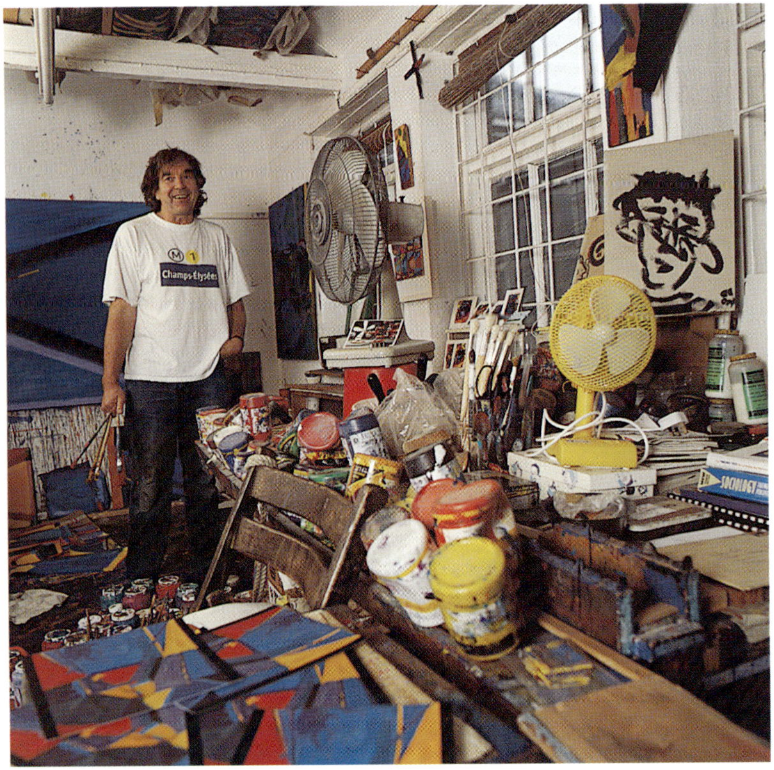

Anthony Frost lives in Morvah and works from a studio in Penzance. The son of Terry Frost, he was born in St Ives in 1951 and studied at Cardiff College of Art. Currently one of his paintings is being translated into a large area of land containing fodder crops at the Eden Project, which will become a living piece of work.

'I've got a beat' - Walking into Turquoise
2000
1220 x 1525mm
acrylic on sailcloth, bedsheet and string
(Steve Tanner)

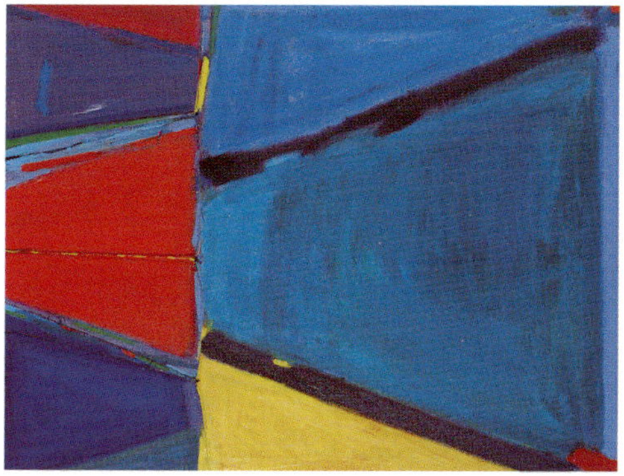

I always wanted to be an artist, there wasn't anything else I was going to do and I know it sounds clichéd but there wasn't anything else I really could do. My dad was a major influence and I remember artists such as David Hockney and Roger Hilton visiting us. Art was all around me and there was no discouragement so it was an easy choice.

I don't know what my intentions are while painting, all I do is paint and I try to keep it as simple as that. My concern is to get it to work colour- and shape-wise and to get the weight right. It's what you see in it, what you bring to it. It's like listening to music; everyone listens to the same sounds and each go away with their own interpretation. I always believed that my work was studio based without outside influences but of course everything is influencing me all the time, whether consciously or not. I think these things are best left unanalysed but I paint wedge shapes because I like that particular shape and it's my shape but as with music people go away with their own interpretation and perhaps see them as sails.

I'd love to show my work more internationally, in fact I'd like to be the top abstract painter in Britain, the World and the Universe. Wherever abstract painting is needed I want people to say there's only one man to go to. Oh, and I'd like a new Rayburn.

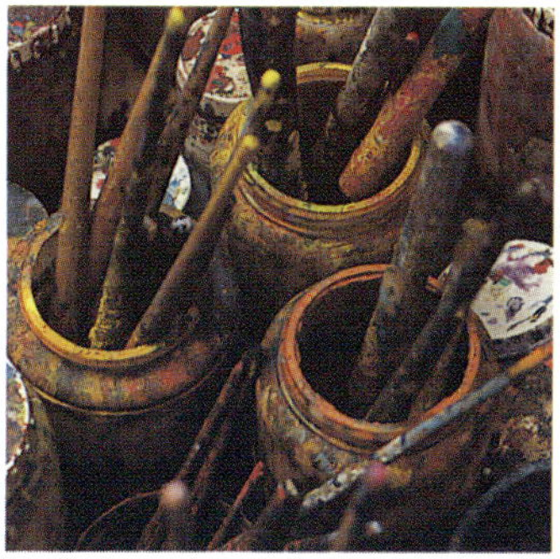

SIR TERRY FROST

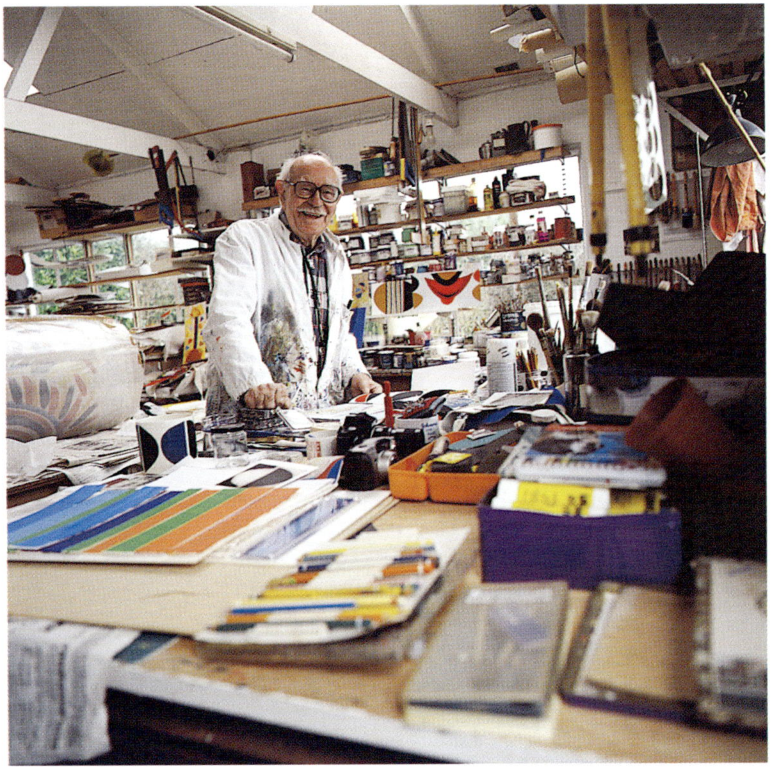

Terry Frost was born in Leamington Spa in 1915. He spent four years as a POW, which is when he first began to paint. He moved to St Ives in 1946 and in the early 1950s worked as an assistant to Barbara Hepworth. He studied at Camberwell School of Art and has taught at various schools and colleges. He moved to Newlyn in 1974 where he still lives and works. He was elected to the Royal Academy in 1998 and received a knighthood in the same year.

Love Tree
2000
1070 x 1070mm
acrylic and collage
(Beaux Arts)

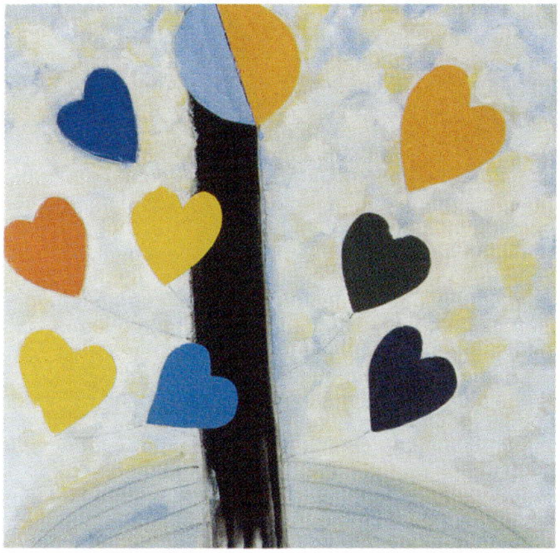

During my wartime experience I was nearly killed several times and saw a lot of my mates die. It made me realise that to do what you want ain't bad and that's when I made up my mind to paint and I've stuck at it ever since.

I learnt a lot about professionalism when I was working for Barbara Hepworth. She was very strict and didn't like anyone gossiping. However, Denis Mitchell and me always had a story to tell one another while we were chipping away at the rough stuff but Barbara could tell from the sound if we were following form. Every stroke has got to make something happen - you move to what you've got to get and if you're not moving to it all the time, you're not working.

Painting keeps me alive. I get a great delight when I think I've done something good and the biggest agony is when nothing comes off at all. Painting stretches emotions and imagination. I'm never ill when I'm in the studio. I can be at home watching the television or reading the paper and I've got aches and pains and I think I'm too old, but I walk over to the studio and after a couple of hours in there I forget that I've ever had a pain of any kind. I think that everybody should do art and everybody can do it and that it's good for the soul. You can cure all kinds of aches and pains with painting - therapeutically it's marvellous.

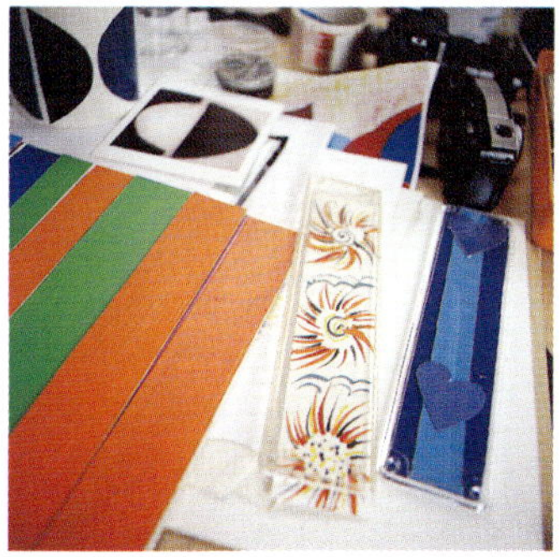

ROSE HILTON

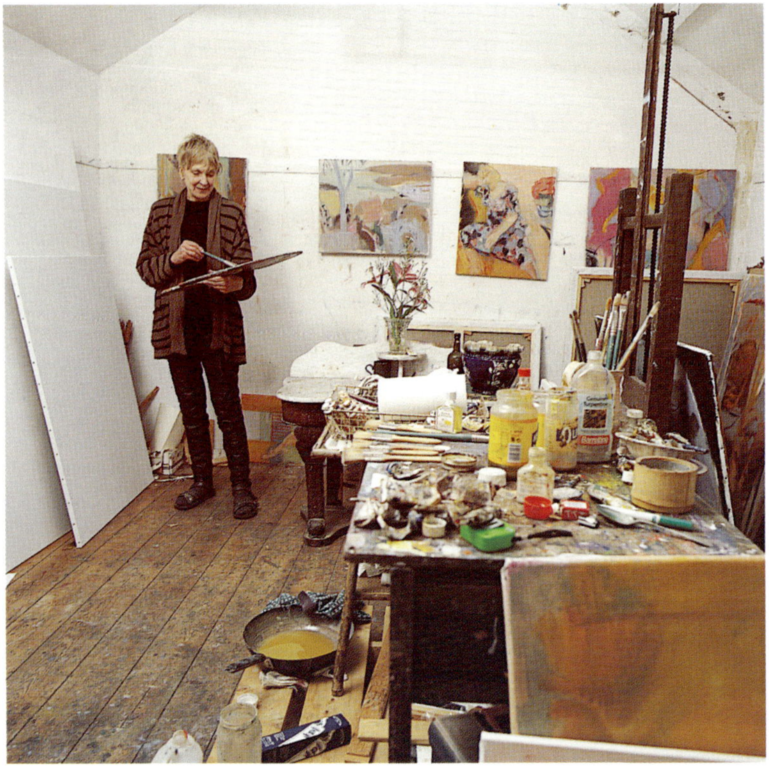

Born in Kent in 1931, Rose Hilton attended Beckenham Art School and the Royal College of Art where she won the Life Drawing and Painting Prize and also the Abbey Miner Scholarship to Rome. In 1965 she married the artist Roger Hilton and settled with their two sons in Botallack, St Just where she still lives. After Roger's death in 1975 she resumed full-time painting.

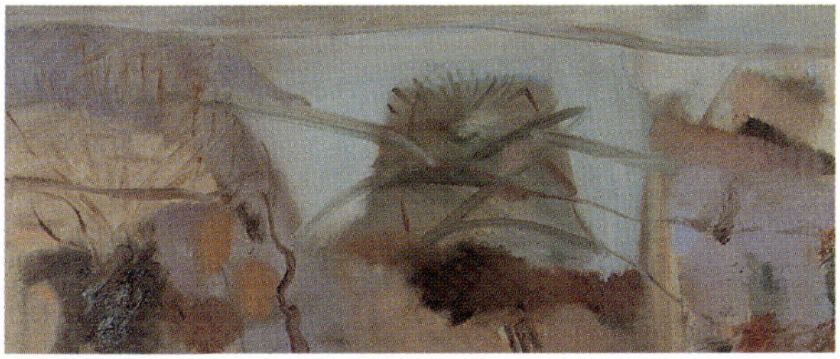

Landscape
2001
400 x 915mm
oil on canvas

Although life with Roger was often difficult, he was an intelligent, witty and charming person, so life was not boring. I didn't paint as we had two young children but I was never very far removed from the whole activity of painting therefore it wasn't all that difficult for me to pick up again when he died.

It took me about ten years to find my style with confidence, which was more or less how I'd been painting at the Royal College. I wasn't directly influenced by Roger because he was an abstract artist but I was impressed by his very accurate use of colour. Using the subject as a vehicle for colour and form is really important for me. I start with a subject because I'm not a completely abstract artist; I like a bit of reality in my pictures, but I tend to use it as a vehicle for making shapes relate to each other and colours bounce off against each other.

I love the fact that I can go to my studio and see the world as I see it through my pictures and it gives me pleasure, if some of the paintings have worked just to look at them. Whether one likes it or not, energy does diminish so I can't always put the hours in that I used to. Now I've got the confidence I want to do bigger paintings and I have four six-foot canvases waiting for me which will be a challenge.

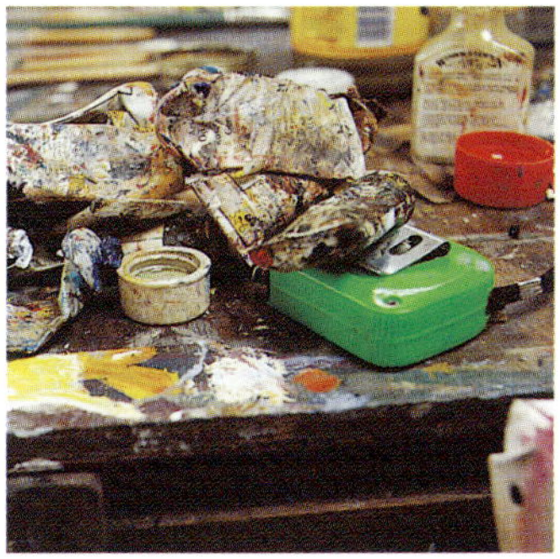

SAX IMPEY

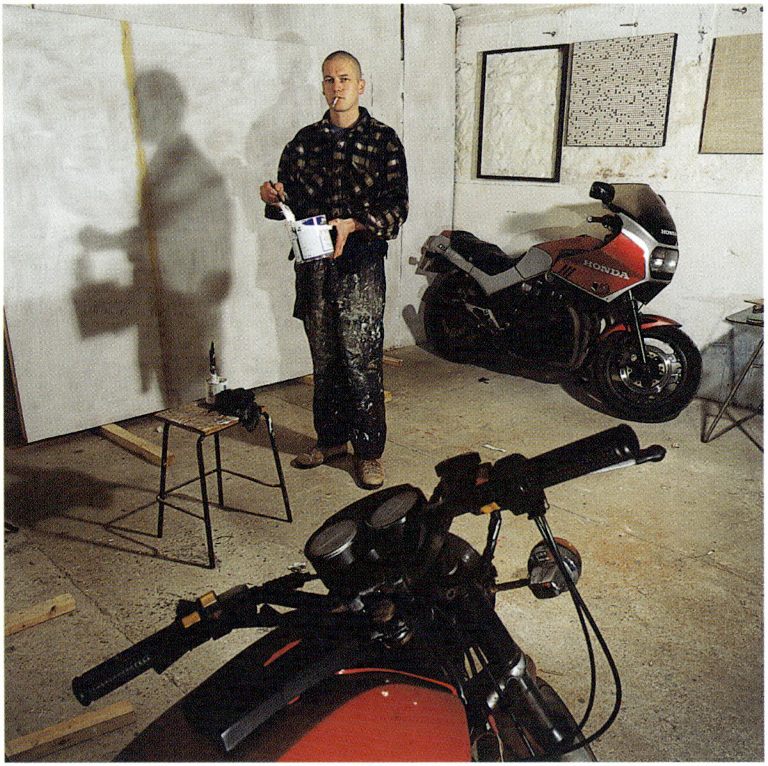

Born in Penzance in 1969, Sax Impey studied Fine Art at Newport. After graduating in 1991, he was involved in various film, theatre and performance projects and travelled in East Africa. He returned to Cornwall in 1994 and now works from a studio at Trencrom Hill near St Ives.

'00.10'
2000
1000 x 1000mm
mixed media

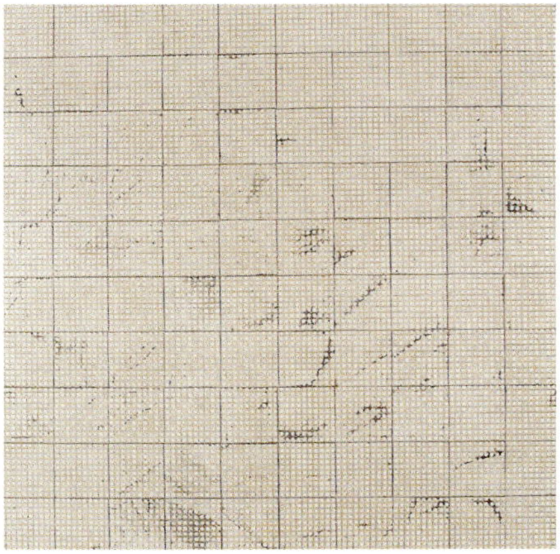

I am currently making works composed of the repetition of movements and elements. The rigorous application of a procedure allied to the introduction of chance, images which are records of the process of their construction. I often begin with monoprints - making composite images of many prints as the first of several processes a piece will undergo. The surface is covered in scored or printed lines, in repeated images, in marks, thousands, tens of thousands, hundreds of thousands of times. This began with a piece called 'October' produced in 1998, which is a seminal piece which has been generating work ever since.

It's important to me that the work is exhibited. That's not to say I'm demonstrating anything - it's a journey, not a demonstration. But an unseen piece of work is impotent, a sterile object and only half the story. It is precisely within the relationship between maker, object and viewer that art exists. Having said that, working here can make exhibiting difficult. The spaces are few and far between; West Cornwall is a long way from everywhere and perhaps as a consequence you can sometimes end up working in something of a vacuum. There is also the assumption that all artists in Cornwall will make landscape-based work - as if all those other issues of human concern don't exist here amongst the natural beauty and the cream teas.

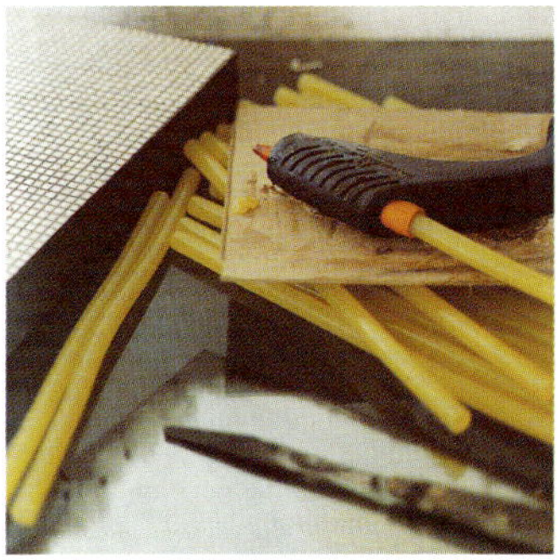

KURT JACKSON

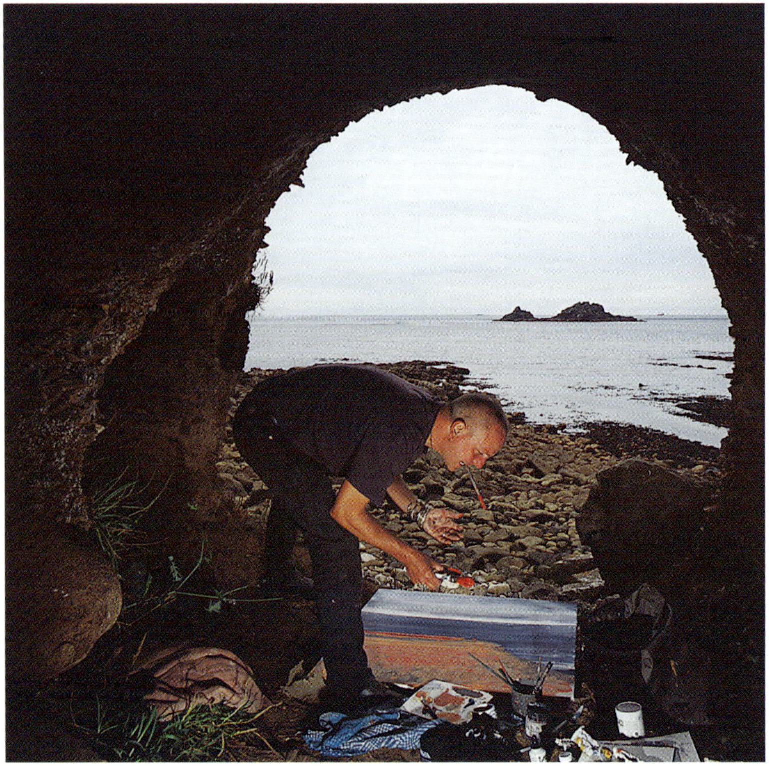

Born in 1961 in Dorset, Kurt Jackson's art training came mainly from his parents who are both artists. He attended art classes at Ruskin College whilst studying Zoology at St Peter's College, Oxford. He has raised thousands of pounds for charities through auctions of his work in London and has appeared in Channel 4's 'Watercolour Challenge' programme. He lives near St Just with Caroline and their three children.

Dusk, Hayle, Storm
2001
230 x 270mm
mixed media

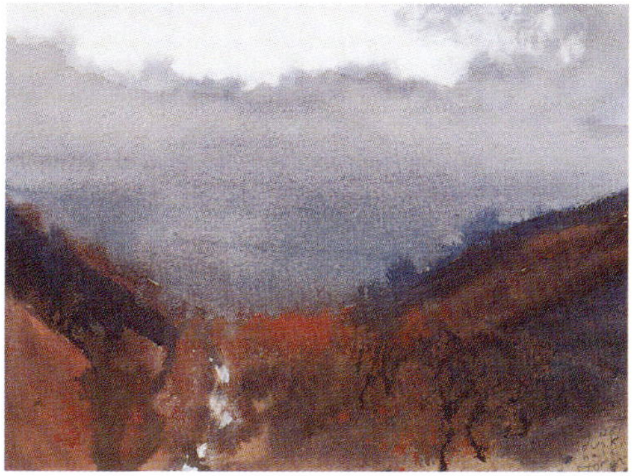

Sometimes living in Penwith feels like living on an island. The landscape where I live has got the coast, moors, valleys and perhaps a woodland if I go looking for it. It's an area where nature hasn't been totally obliterated; every field seems to have a little rough corner left and that landscape attracts me.

The real kick for me is in painting outdoors. It's a totally different experience to painting in the studio. There are a number of different factors to my painting: there's the actual putting the paint on the surface of the canvas and trying to capture what I'm looking at. There's also the more subtle side of what I'm feeling, hearing and smelling - the atmosphere. When you move into a studio, some of these things are missing and you deal more with materials and an idea.

Ideally I like to have all factors happening at once but sometimes it's fun just to get totally immersed in paint. I try not to work at weekends when I'm with the family but I nearly always have a sketchbook with me in my pocket. If I'm in a shop and the kids are buying shoes then I'll draw them trying on shoes or if I'm buying a pound of beetroot then I might draw that! The ideal is to draw every minute of the day because it's all fascinating.

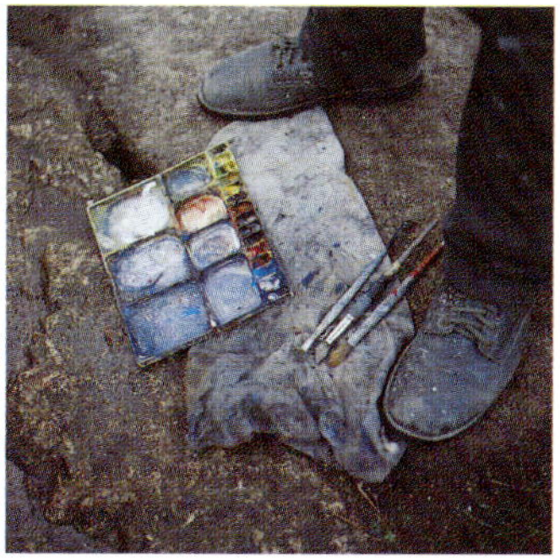

GRAHAM JOBBINS

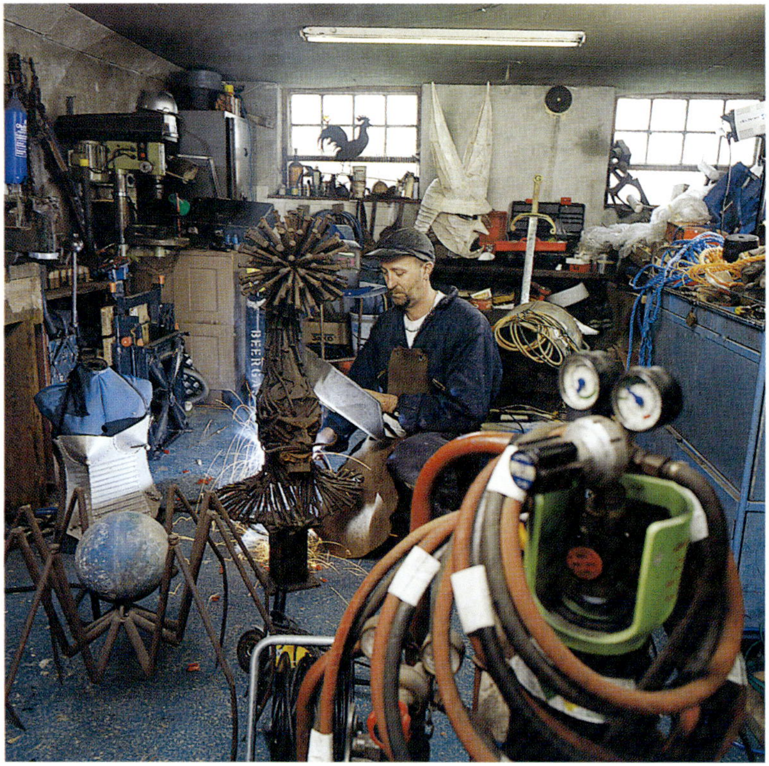

Born in Kent in 1959, Graham Jobbins studied sculpture at Maidstone College of Art. He moved to Cornwall in 1958 and in conjunction with exhibiting metalwork sculptures in galleries, he produces large-scale constructions for theatrical and festival events.

Running Dog
1999
600 x 500mm
scrap steel

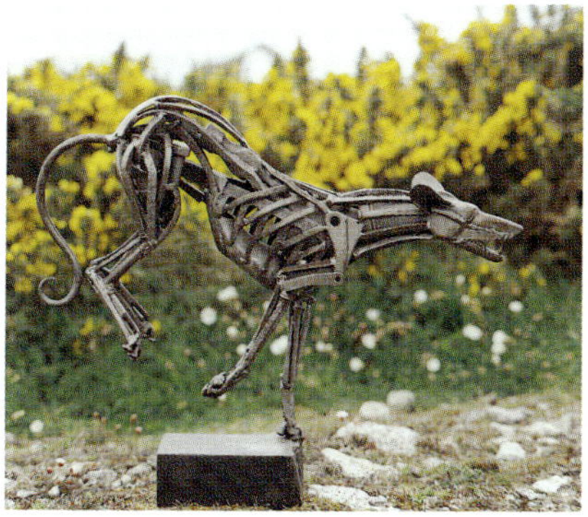

At art school I was tutored by Anthony Gormley, working with him on his early lead 'Body' sculptures. We also collaborated on a land-drawing project using rocks and other natural materials creating giant drawings, made to be viewed from the air.

I am very interested in anatomy, with a fascination for dissection; I find the realistic drawings of Stubbs extremely beautiful. I use scrap metal and junk items to construct my mainly figurative work, with a preference for dogs and insects. My largest piece to date is a three metre high 'Iron Man', which was purchased by Pete Townsend, founder member of 'The Who'. Other influences are images sourced from science fiction, from other sculptors such as Jacob Epstein and of course, walking my dog.

Recently most of my 'bread and butter' work has been creating huge animated processional sculptures. These demonstrate a completely different art form, contacting a whole new audience, many of which may never have stepped inside an art gallery. I derive great pleasure from the awe-struck gasps and spontaneous applause that receive my 'Giants' as they parade through the streets on St Just's Lafrowda Day and Penzance's Mazey Day. I feel the community I live in is proud of the work I do for these fantastic festivals.

I often work with the sculptor David Kemp, assisting him with many projects and I am a regular maker for Truro's 'City of Lights'. I have been commissioned by Kneehigh Theatre to make set pieces for several of their productions and I was the set designer for the acclaimed 'Origo Mundi' (part 1 of the Ordinalia Cycle) play staged in St Just's Plen an Gwary in 2000. I'm looking forward to more diversity in my future work.

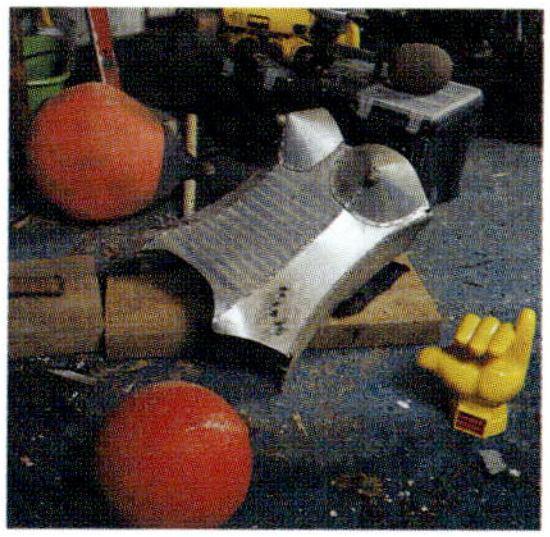

ROBERT JONES

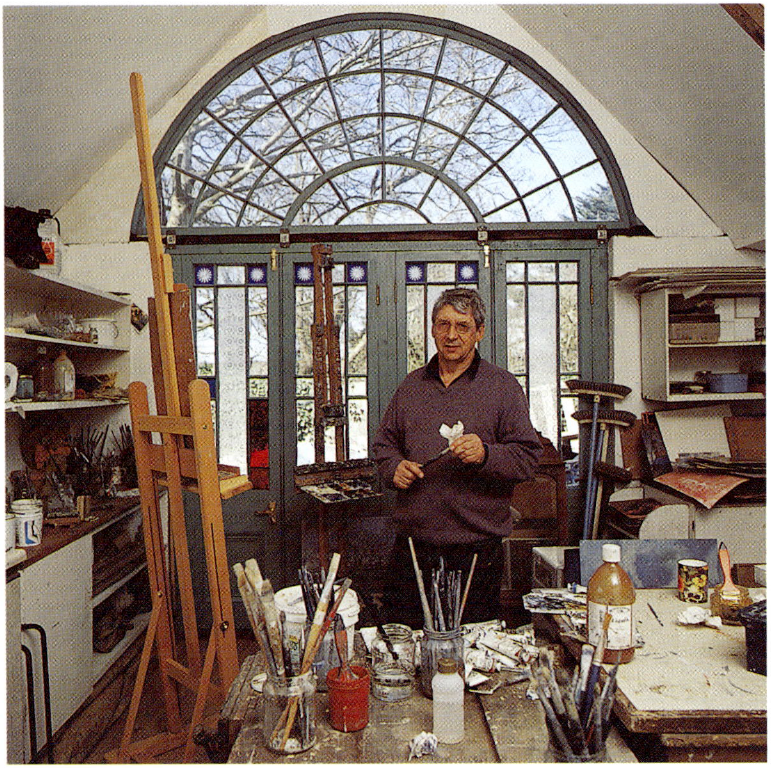

Robert Jones was born and brought up in Cornwall. He attended Falmouth School of Art in the early 1960s and later, taught at Summerhill School in Suffolk, returning to Cornwall with his family in the early 1970s. He then spent several years as skipper of fishing boats working around the west coast of Cornwall. Throughout his time at sea and during a subsequent period of teaching at Mullion School and Falmouth College of Art, he continued to draw, paint and exhibit his work.

antic Surf St Ives
0
x 590mm
on board

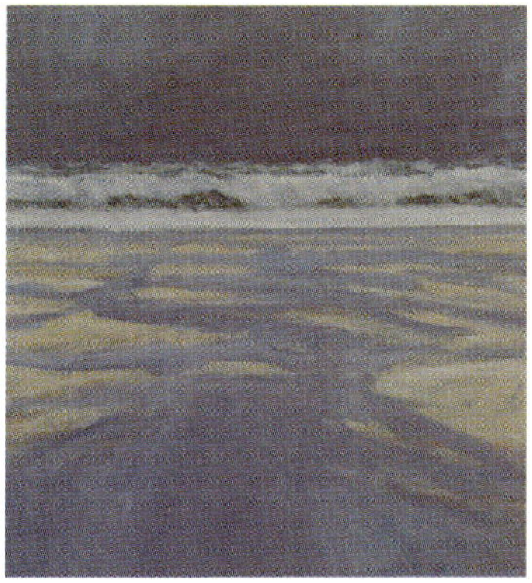

I have always had two methods of working. One is in the studio from memory and imagination; the other is to take my paints and go and sit in the landscape usually working on smaller spontaneous paintings. This process of working has a different sort of life to it, an energy which I try to capture and which comes from working quickly.

I paint every day for weeks and weeks and feel a contentment and involvement which isn't there during the periods when I cannot work at all. I enjoy working on one-man exhibitions and was pleased to have my drawings exhibited in the Hayward, and a dozen paintings in the Tate, St Ives, but the most satisfaction comes from hearing people who own my paintings and appreciate them. I met a man the other day who said 'I bought a painting of yours and at the time I didn't even know who it was by, but I pass that painting every day and it gives me pleasure every time I walk past it'.

It makes you realise that people appreciate what you do and value it; that my painting will remain on someone's wall long after I have gone, and will continue to tell its story.

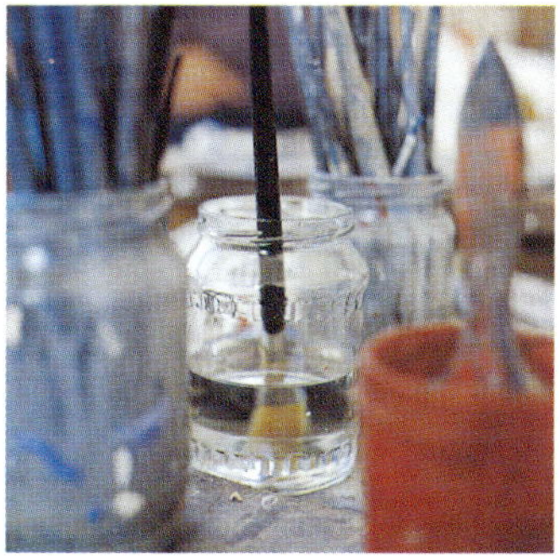

RACHAEL KANTARIS

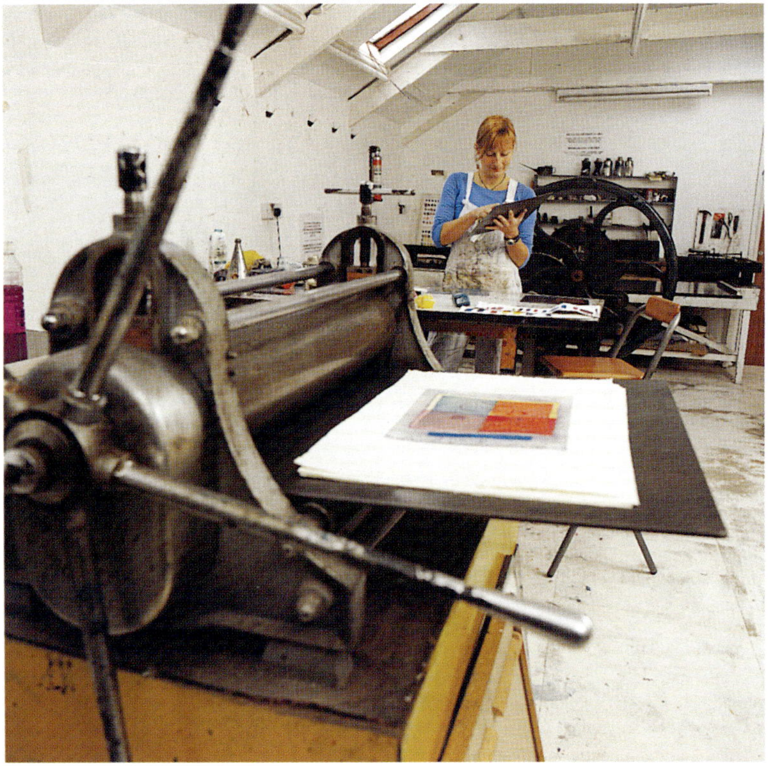

Born in Australia in 1967, Rachael Kantaris moved to Britain when she was four. She studied at Falmouth School of Art and Brighton University. After graduating she travelled widely, working in studios in Berlin and Melbourne. In 1997 she was invited by the British Council to have an exhibition of contemporary printmaking in Manila, and whilst there she taught at the University of the Philippines. She lives in St Ives and runs the Porthmeor Print Workshop.

Fine Line
2001
300 x 350mm
artist's proof
etching

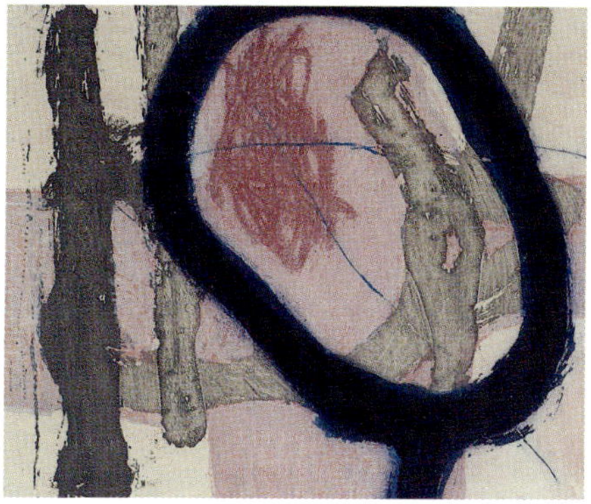

When I first discovered etching I saw the potential for exploring my fascination for colour and fell in love with the medium. It's less direct than painting and allows an element of both chance and control. It's also a very physical medium - somewhere between sculpture and painting. I love the contradiction of making textures on metal which end up as painterly marks on paper. However, I sometimes feel constricted which is why I have recently begun painting again as well as printmaking.

Each piece of work is like an adventure, and I don't know until I get there where it's going to end up. I never make a piece of work which is a replica of a sketch, it's much more of an ongoing dialogue which forms in the push and pull of the process. I'm a perfectionist when it comes to colour and often use so many that it can be very time consuming - there's no short cut and it might take an hour or two to ink up the plates each time I change a colour slightly. Sometimes this proofing stage can take weeks until I'm completely happy with it, but what's lovely is that none of this struggle shows and the final piece has a freshness about it. It can be quite labour intensive, but the excitement of working on the plates outweighs this. When my work's going well it changes my whole perception of life and I suppose that's why I do it - because it's incredibly exciting - especially with etching, there's something magical when you pull the final image off the press and you've got it right.

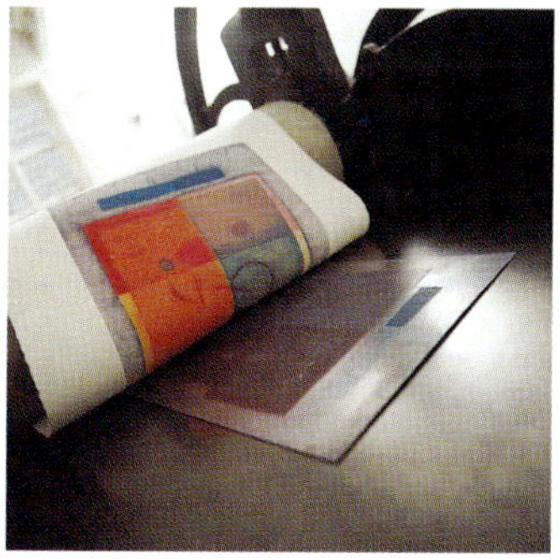

DAVID KEMP

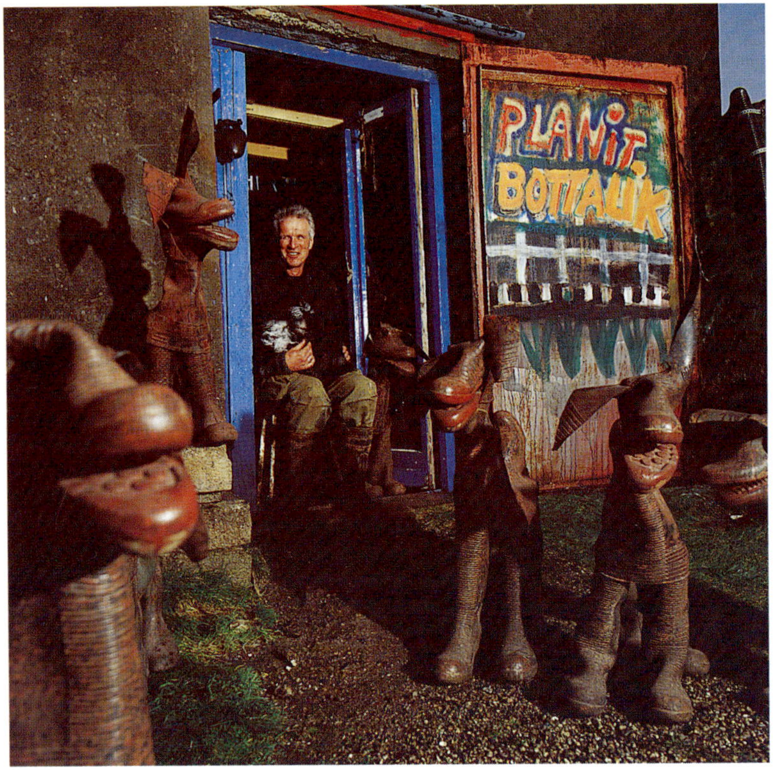

Born in London in 1945, David Kemp studied at Farnham and Wimbledon Schools of Art. He came to live near St Just in 1972 and has collected junk dumped in the landscape to assemble works that illustrate his interest in telling stories and communicating ideas. His work has been shown in museums and public galleries throughout Britain including the Tate Gallery, St Ives. His ‘Art of Darkness’ museum at Botallack featured in the 1997 ‘Quality of Light’ international arts event, and his recent commissions include ‘Brian’s walk-through Brain’ at the Lowry in Salford and the ‘Tropics Trader’ at the Eden Project. He has also collaborated with Kneehigh Theatre on several ‘Landscape Theatre’ projects in Cornwall and abroad.

Chain Gang
height 250mm
anchor chain and
mattocks

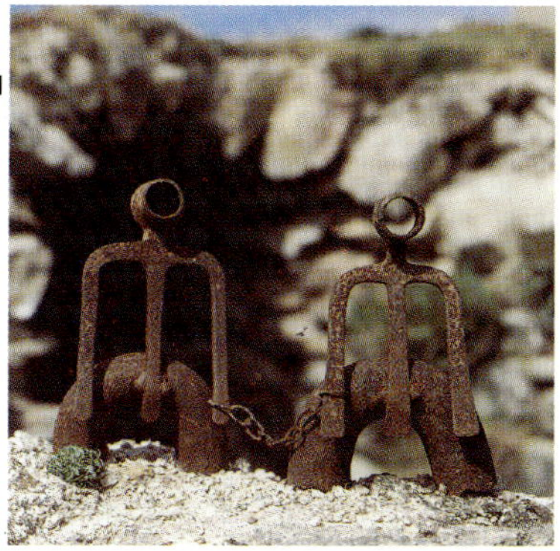

I have lived on the Tinners' Coast for nearly thirty years. The ruined mines and post-industrial landscape have always had a very strong influence on my work, both small and large scale. On the ruined landscapes of the Durham Moors, I built huge post-industrial heads - the Old Transformers and King Coal, from derelict machinery on the sites of old mines and steelworks. In Cornwall I often work like some sort of future archaeologist and assemble collections of 'Relics from the Late Iron Age' which have been displayed in public museums as 'Troves of spurious archaeological Treasures', making entertaining connections between new technologies and old mythologies.
I started making things out of junk years ago because it was free and readily available. Our lives are full of things and what we throw away says as much about us as the objects we keep. The cluttered 'language of things' is full of clues that tell stories about ourselves and the way we live. I am very interested in finding ways of putting objects in front of people that might communicate ideas about the place we share. Some things are funny and some are frightening.

The things that we make are changing the world.

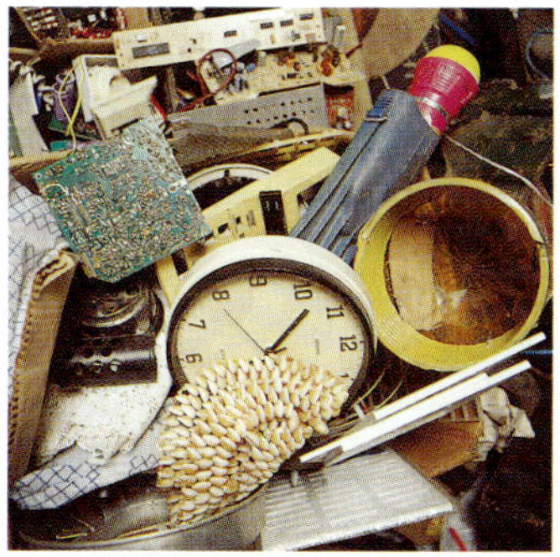

JEREMY Le GRICE

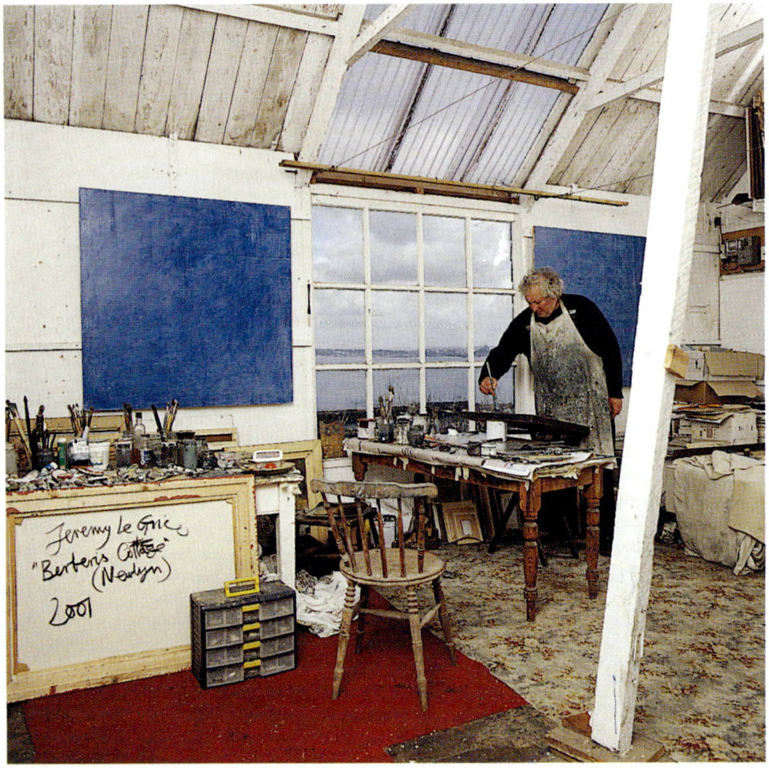

Jeremy Le Grice was born in 1936 on a journey towards Penzance from London. He studied at Peter Lanyon's Summer School in St Ives and then the Slade. His career as a painter began whilst living in St Just. In the early seventies he moved to Gloucestershire to teach, returning to paint in West Penwith in 1983.

Hull
2000
500 x 500mm
oil on board

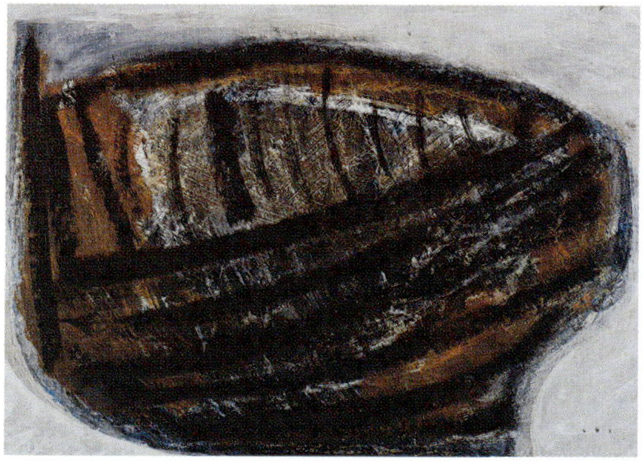

I became committed to painting aged seven when I won a competition. The painting was of a sailor in front of a firing battleship whose smoke smothers St. Michael's Mount. In front of this baptism of fire, ironically, he wears a broad grin. This putative self-portrait appeared in many newspapers, providing a powerful feel-good factor at an early age.

At seventeen I met Peter Lanyon having discovered his 'Harvest Festival' hanging in Newlyn Gallery; it seemed the truest painting I had ever seen. We were friends for the last eight years of his life. He taught at two successive Summer Schools, giving his knowledge to the students unreservedly. It was a ball. Every day intensive, fast-track learning, so different from the usual art college yawn. Under his favourite slogan 'up the rebels', art, girls and landscape fell into place - experiencing creativity in the raw. Those blue days and bright nights in St Ives, represent the fifties for me. He opened another door: London and the Slade.

Another seminal moment occurred in my early thirties, seeing a notice attached to the rigging of a Baltic schooner: 'Return fare paid from Los Angeles'. I leapt on deck. Over the Atlantic, up the Pacific Coast - one of six - whales breaking the surface in the trade winds, their skins clustered with barnacles and songs echoing through deep-blue ocean space. Seize the day.

When artists strike it right unforgettable images emerge. That is the spontaneity, gamble and unpredictability that underlies every creative act. My life entails acquiring knowledge to make valid images, then letting them go in order to make others.

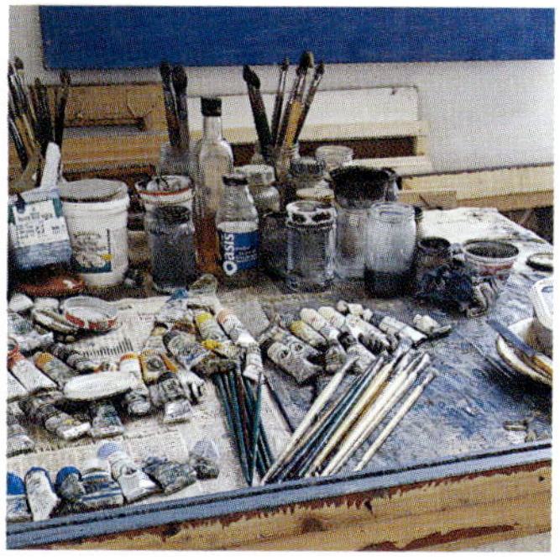

ALEXANDER MACKENZIE

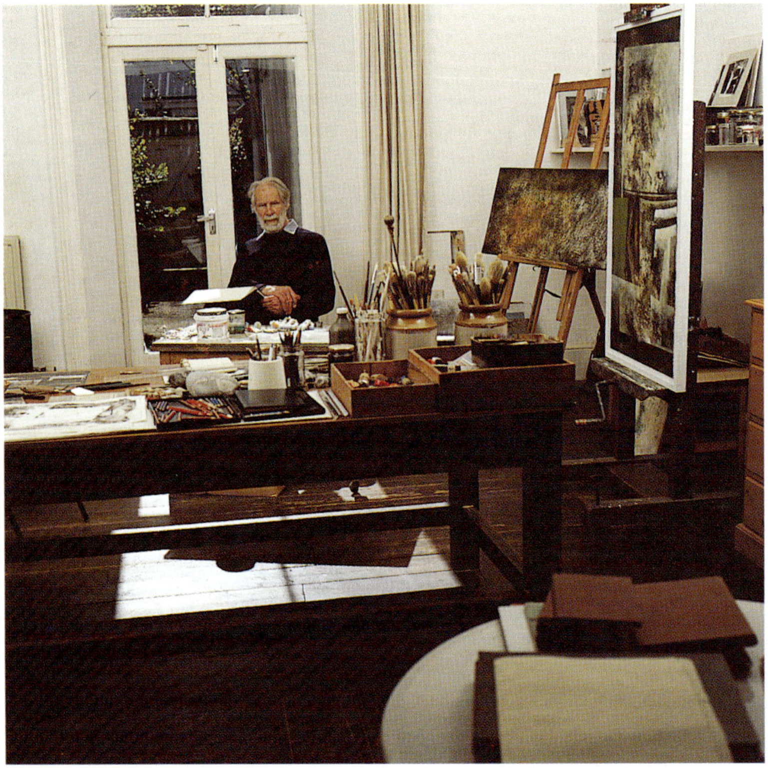

Alexander Mackenzie's work can be found in collections worldwide including that of the Tate Gallery, London and the Arts Council of Great Britain. Born in Liverpool in 1923, he studied at Liverpool College of Art and moved to Cornwall in 1951. He was appointed Head of Fine Art at Plymouth Art College in 1964. He lives and works in Penzance.

Granite Continent
2000
1220 x 610mm
oil on board

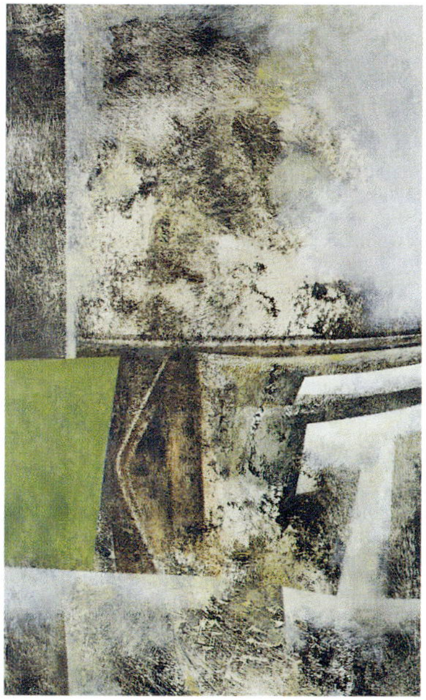

Although essentially abstract, my work contains many references to visual qualities in the landscape: line, form, texture and colour as well as sensations of space, volume and structure. Most have their origins in visual experience although emotional and intellectual demands must always be resolved.

The degree of abstraction is part of the complex and mysterious creative process, which is essentially intuitive, being a search for visual equivalents of feelings and sensations evoked by the landscape.

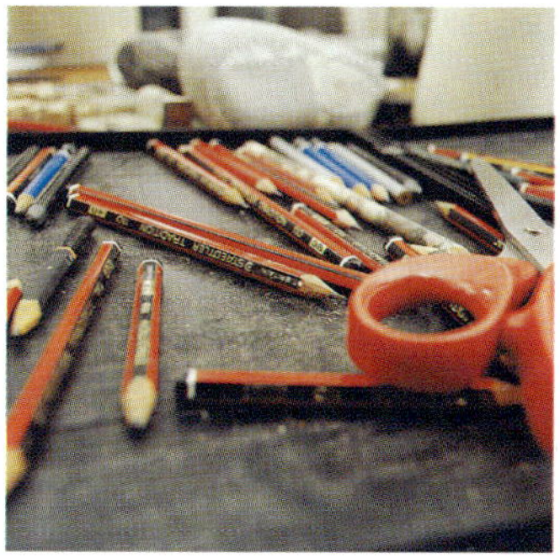

DAPHNE McCLURE

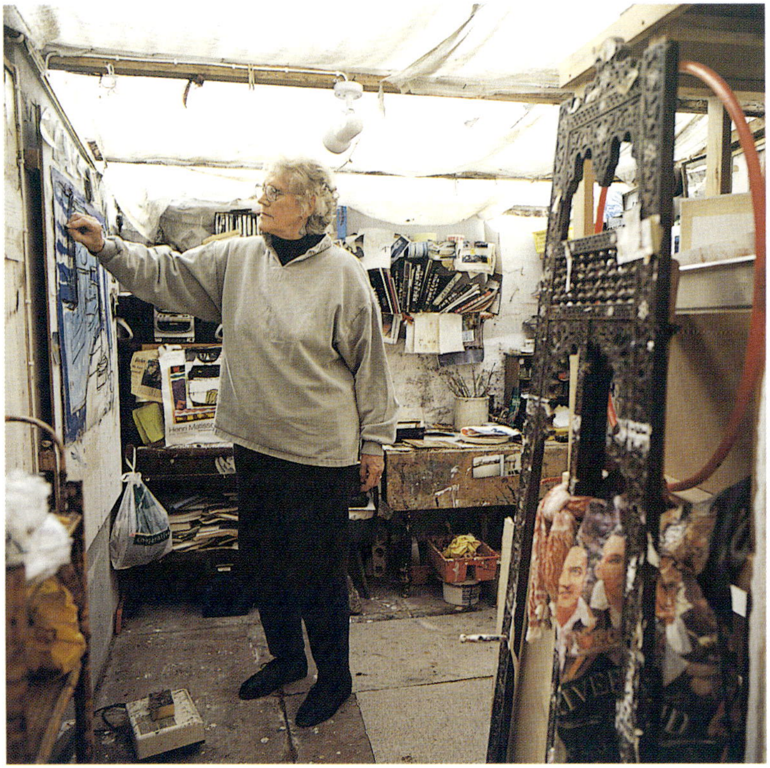

Daphne McClure was born in Helston and studied at Hornsey College and the Central School of Art. She returned to Cornwall with her family in 1976 and now lives in Penzance. In 1995 she was commissioned by the Tate, St Ives to design a mug to coincide with the first ever exhibition at the gallery.

Newlyn Bridges
2001
500 x 815mm
mixed media on board

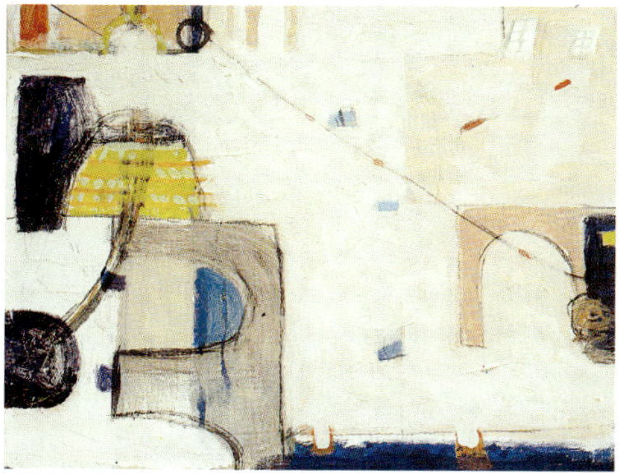

When you're Cornish I think it's difficult to live elsewhere. It's so beautiful to live here and the whole of the twenty-five years I was away from Cornwall I was disorientated so I came back to live in Porthleven.

I thought it was going to be wonderful to paint but I found it difficult because the image of Peter Lanyon's painting of Porthleven was always in my mind. I was so disappointed, I gave up painting for a couple of years and opened an antiques shop. Then a friend who took aerial photographs gave me a photograph of Porthleven and that was it. Suddenly I could see these great shapes and I could paint them and I did so for the next ten years. I used to take a sketchbook with me when I went abroad but soon realised I could only paint Cornwall. I don't know why that is but I suppose at the back of my mind, it's only Cornwall that matters.

I come to the studio every day but the painting's got to be as right as I can get it before I will show it anywhere. In my painting I'm quite a perfectionist. I paint because I love it and I like the challenges it brings. I look back at all the paintings I've ever done and realise they just poured out of me, but when you get older you haven't got as much time or energy to pursue it. I know what I still want out of my paintings but it doesn't come as fast as it used to.

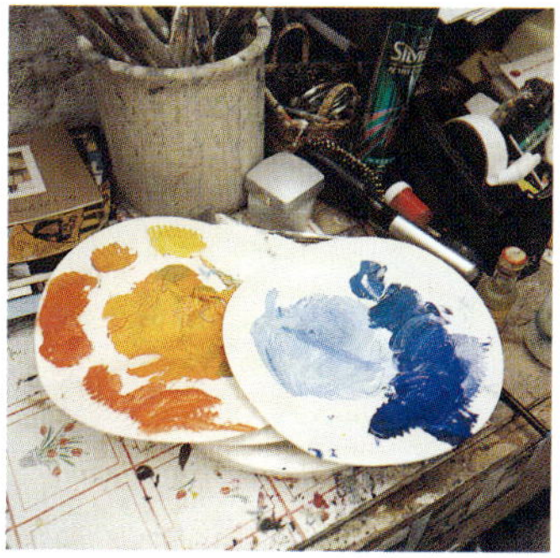

MARGO MAECKELBERGHE

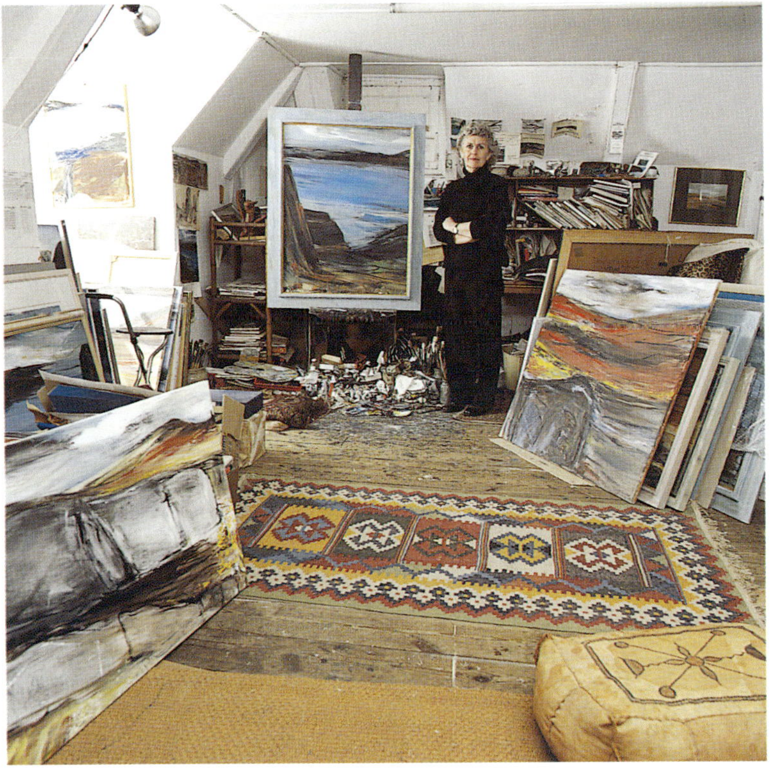

Cornish born and bred, Margo Maeckelberghe studied at Penzance School of Art, then 1949 at Bath Academy of Art, Corsham where William Scott, Peter Lanyon and Bryan Winter were amongst her tutors. After qualifying in 1952 she taught in London, before living for three years in Gibraltar. In 1959 she returned to Cornwall where she now lives and works. She makes frequent painting trips to Europe, the Americas, Middle and Far East. In 1997 she was made a Bard at the Cornish Gorsedd.

Ancient Land
2000
915 x 1000mm
oil on canvas

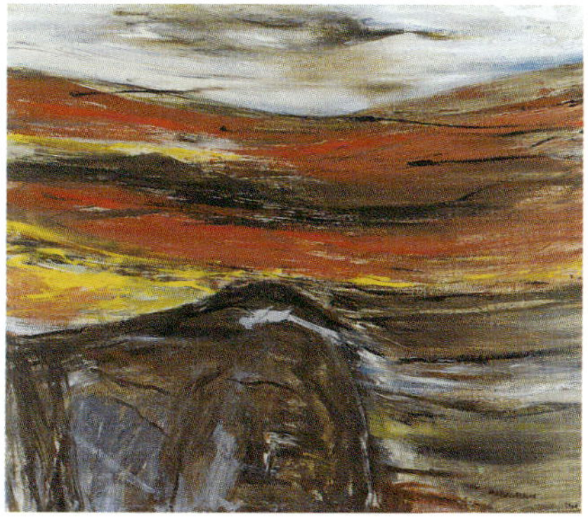

Painting for me is a passion. The moors, seas and rocks of Cornwall provide me with inexhaustible painting material. Always there is this peculiar clarity of light, throwing the landscape of Penwith into sharp perspective. It is a land of great antiquity, primeval, sometimes savage, powerful and to me magical.

I make many drawings, sketches and colour references on site - often 'en-plein air' but once back in the studio these are only starting points. Images change, develop and lead into new variations - one constantly goes to the edge, abstracting, selecting, rejecting again and again colours and shapes in an effort to recreate with paint on canvas space, movement and matter. This process is not straightforward - the world of the painter is not the sinecure that many imagine. It is often a struggle between intense pleasure and frustration - the 'noir incertitude' of Stendhal.

Sometimes, to escape this painful process I make excuses to avoid starting, I tidy the studio, clean the brushes, sort out my palette of it's spectrum of paints, but once I start to paint, the work takes over. Like a drug, it is addictive and one has to beware of complacency - of falling into the trap of repetitive clichés.

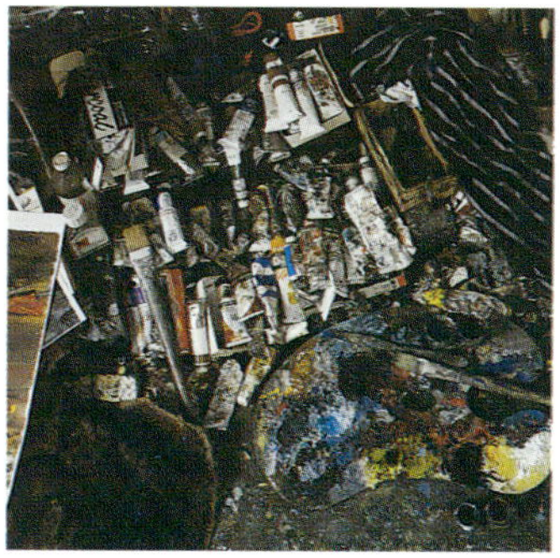

MAGGIE MATTHEWS

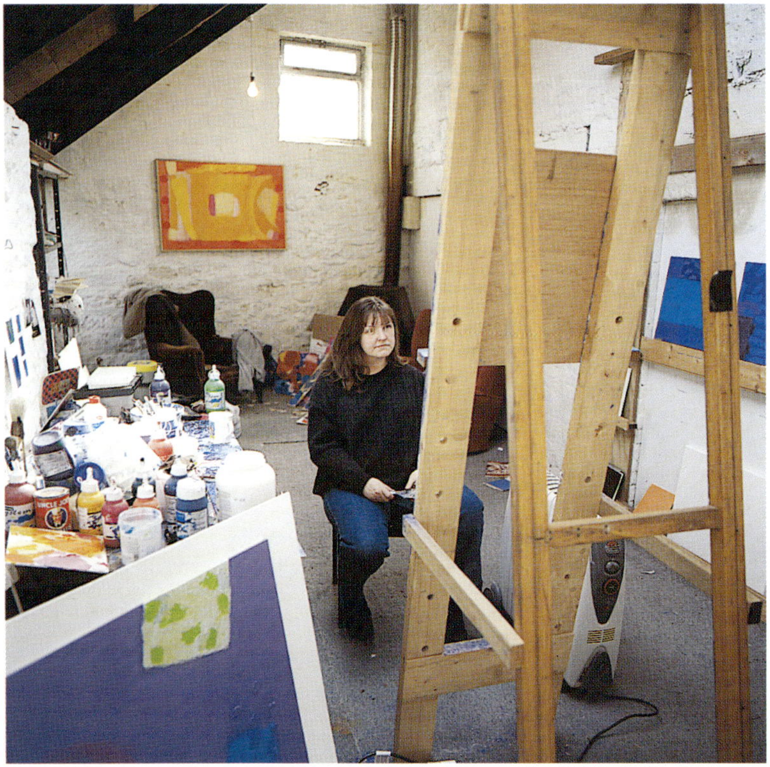

Born in Wales in 1964, Maggie Matthews studied at Newport Art College and Exeter College of Art and Design. Moving to West Penwith in 1988, she now lives in Botallack with her daughter and has a studio in Newlyn.

Between Wind and Water
2001
410 x 410mm
acrylic on canvas

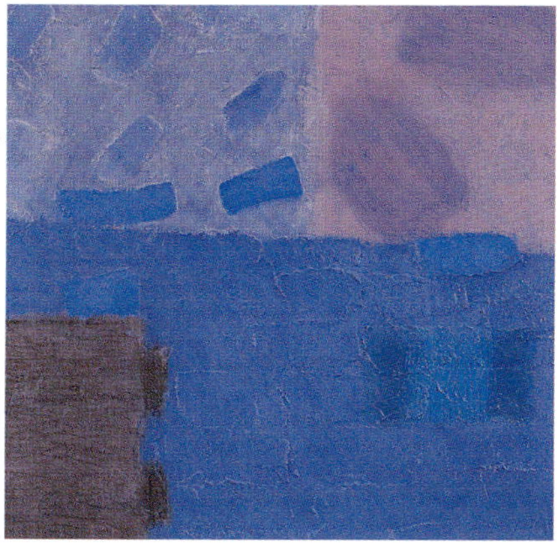

My paintings are mostly concerned with the sea and the sky, the land itself has been reduced to islands of form hanging in space. I walk on the cliffs, find a sheltered spot and spend the day sketching, arranging the scene until something excites me. My colours are not naturalistic or symbolic, simply intuitive, expressing how I feel. Taking the ideas back to the studio I pull out the compositions and paint them over and over until there's a point where it works.

I was brought up in the Welsh mountains, and as a child had great freedom to walk across moors, down caves, in the valleys and over hill tops, and that has given me a real love for landscape. In Cornwall I am drawn to the sea and spellbound by the interplay of elemental forces, the constantly changing richness of life itself.

I feel so lucky being able to work and paint here, and I'd be lying if I said I wasn't totally thrilled when someone buys a painting. I hope people can take my work home and feel that it adds something to their lives, paintings are there for people to build relationships with.

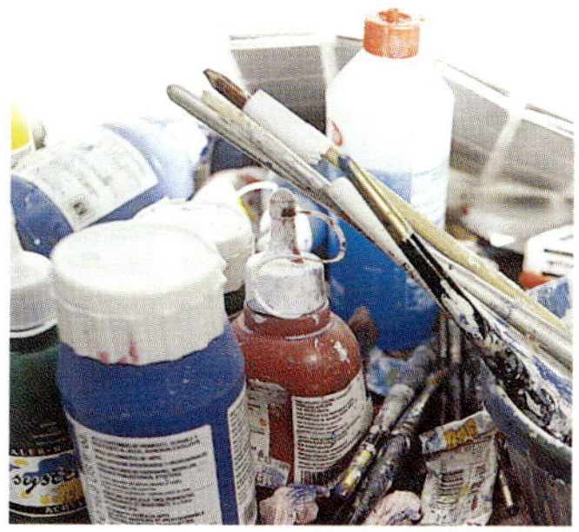

JUNE MILES

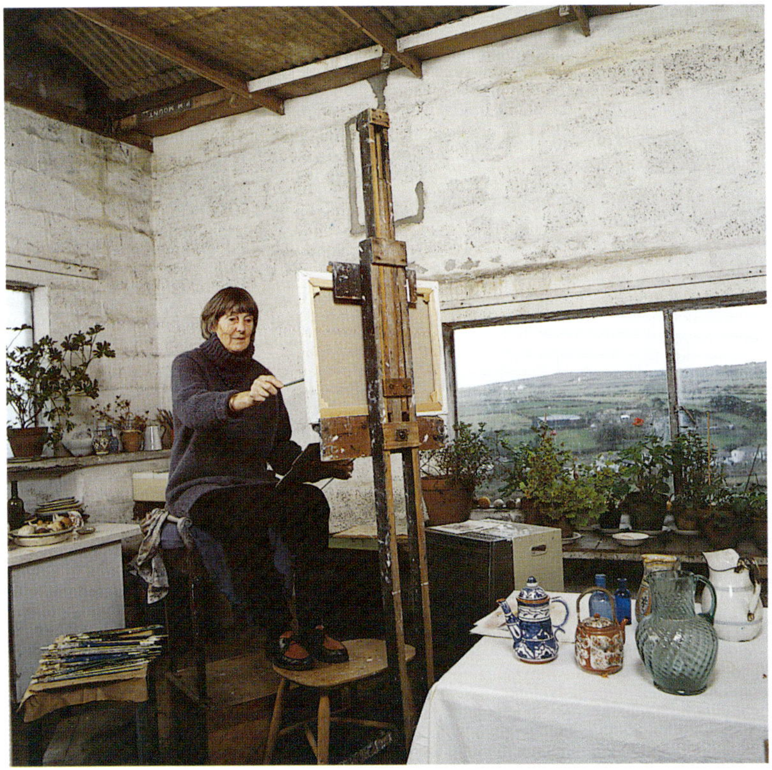

June Miles was born in London in 1924 and spent the first six years of her life on an island near Hong Kong. She studied at the Slade and during the war drew maps in an Admiralty drawing office. She lives in St Just with her husband Paul Mount.

Cyclamen
2000
500 x 500mm
oil on canvas

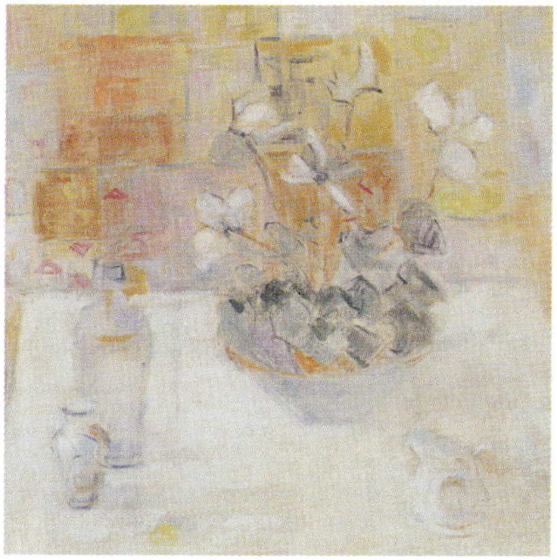

I married the painter Paul Feiler at the end of the war and moved to Bristol where our three children were born. At the start of my art career I was painting portraits in Bristol and landscapes in Cornwall where we had a second home. When my marriage to Paul Feiler ended I moved to Cornwall and concentrated on landscape painting for the next ten years, commuting to teach at the Bristol Polytechnic and the Bristol Folk House. The subject of still lifes didn't become a feature of my work until much later when I married Paul Mount in 1978 and ceased commuting to Bristol, so my collection of still life objects which had been used in teaching, became mine to use. The return of these, combined with finding an old mirror, began my fascination with still life.

Connections interest me - the relationship of buildings to their surroundings, or flowers and objects to the cloth on which they stand. The reflected image creates an illusion of depth whilst at the same time doesn't lose the sense of the picture plane. My paintings are not planned, they evolve as I work directly onto the canvas without using sketches.

I think I have always been visually aware and remember attending evening drawing classes at the age of thirteen. Painting, it seems to me, is about trying to solve problems that one has set for oneself and sometimes it seems like self imposed torture; but being stuck with oneself, inevitably one keeps trying.

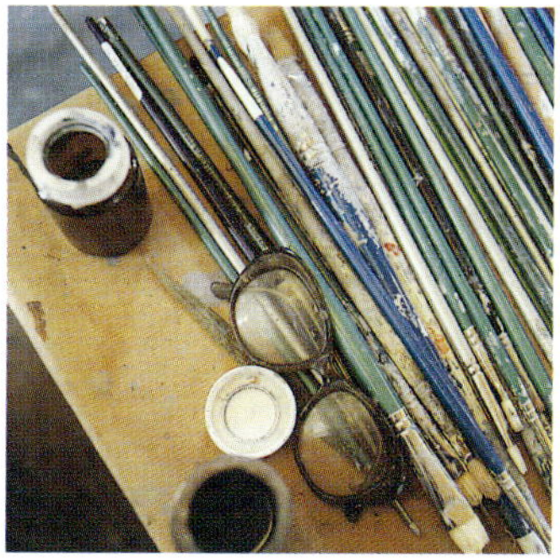

JOHN MILLER

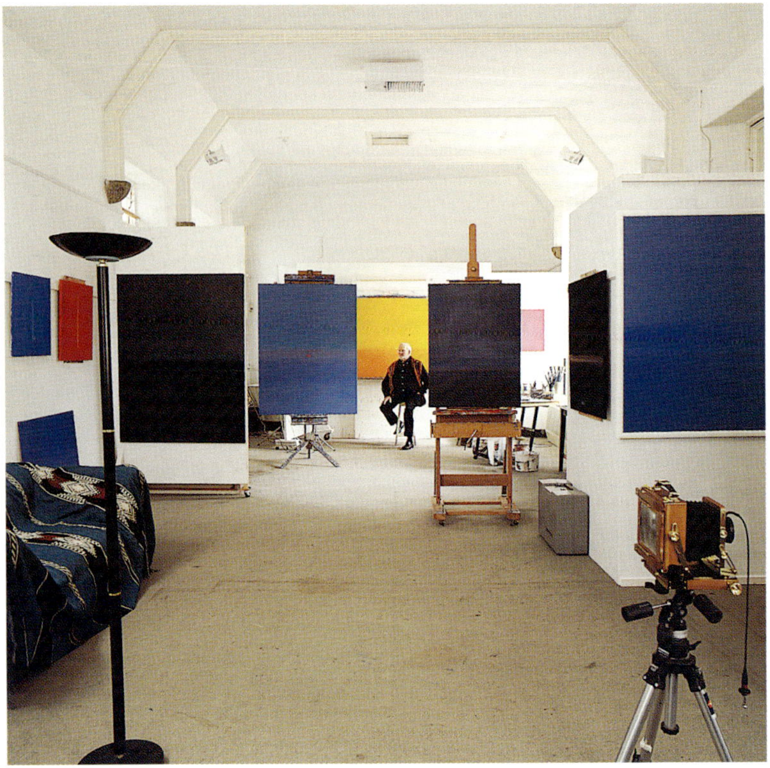

Born in London in 1931, John Miller was involved in theatre and films before studying architecture in London in 1952. He moved to Cornwall in 1958 and his studio is now based in Penzance. He is a lay canon of Truro Cathedral where he has a painting 'Cornubia - Land of the Saints'. His most recent commissions include a poster for the London Underground. showing the Tate Modern from across the river Thames.

Dawn Return
2001
315 x 260mm
oil on canvas

The experience of architecture was for me, wonderful. Many people believe that if an architect begins to paint then the work will be concerned only with buildings, but it gave me an insight and a comprehension of scale and space, which I hope comes through in my paintings. I paint every day; I come into the studio or in the summer go to the beach and see something which moves me to paint. I become obsessional about certain subjects and have to paint my way through them. I draw an enormous amount just for the sake of drawing. I draw everything I see especially on the beach, children playing and many things that don't appear in the paintings, but in some way inform them. When it comes to paintings I don't even lay them out, I just start to push the paint around and explore it like that.

I don't know why my work has proved popular. Someone said to me that the work reminds them of being young and Son the beach and it has also been said they give a peaceful feeling - although they are not peaceful to paint. Painting gives me a life. I am a painter who very much wants to share my enjoyment of life. I am not painting for myself - but having said that, it is difficult to know how to share it. I can only celebrate what makes me tick and some people will tune in and some won't. I want to paint what is special for me in the hope that other people will get something from it.

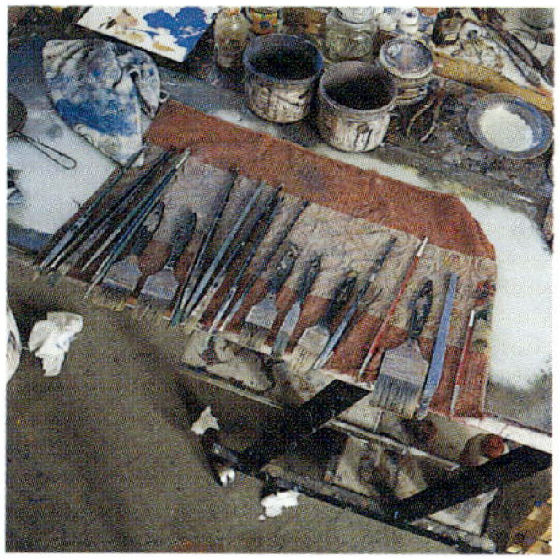

PAUL MOUNT

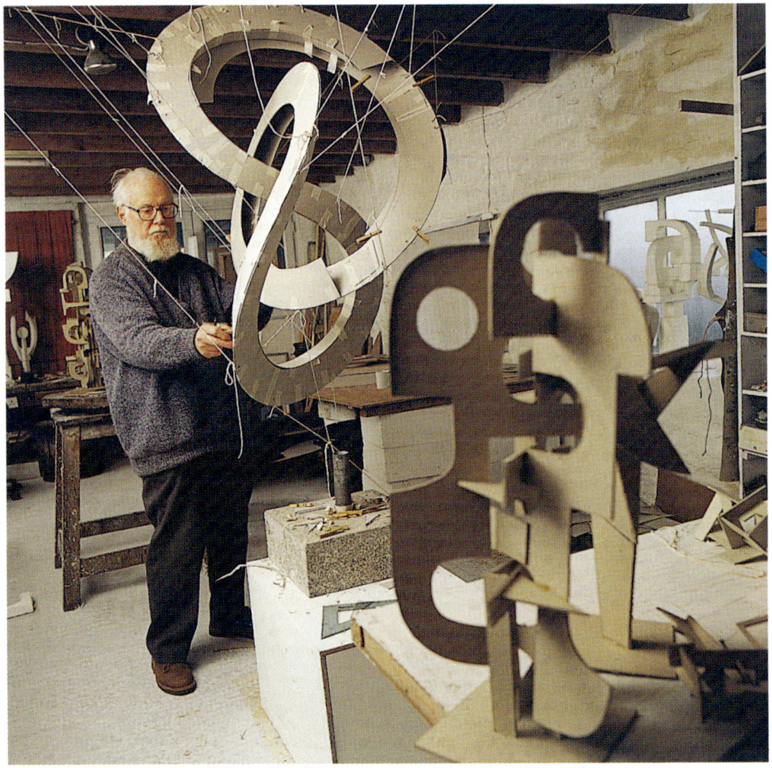

Born in Devon in 1922, Paul Mount studied at the Royal College of Art. He has taught at Winchester School of Art and Yaba College in Nigeria. After six years in West Africa teaching and sculpting he returned to England in 1962 and lives in St Just with his wife June Miles.

El Conjurador
2001
height 150cm
welded
phosphor
bronze

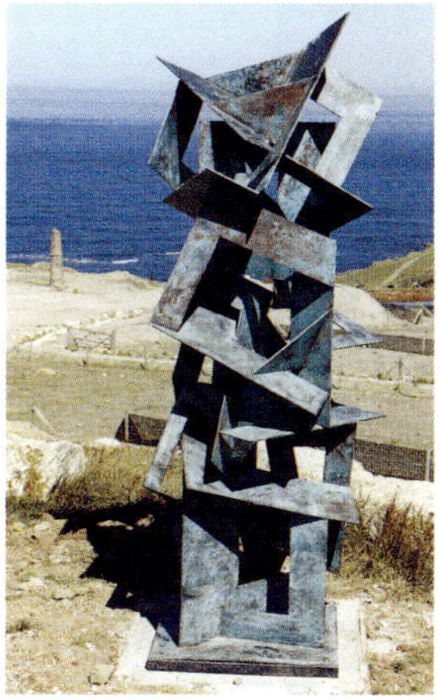

I studied painting at the Royal College and turned to sculpture seven years after my graduation, whilst directing the art department at Yaba College in Nigeria. Carving was one of the few ways in which students could earn a living and I wanted to encourage skills to be developed along traditional lines, but in relation to contemporary demands, so I engaged a Benin carver and learnt from him about the craft. After producing several carved pieces in wood, I decided that it was not the medium for me, I never saw the image in the wood as the African students seemed to do naturally. I wanted to construct in a more flexible medium that allowed for continual redesigning. At this time, I was commissioned by architects in Nigeria to incorporate large scale, inexpensive sculptures for prestige buildings. This required ingenuity in exploiting new materials such as concrete, welded steel and fibreglass and designing abstractly, opening up fresh avenues of thought.

At first I designed on paper, but found this inadequate to describe a whole form and too easy to draw something impossible to construct, so I began using wax, plaster, cardboard or polystyrene models for the finished sculptures of bronze, iron or stainless steel.

The size and scale of my work now varies enormously. I am quite happy working on commissioned projects with the challenges involved, but I no longer do many and enjoy the consequent freedom, keeping several pieces going simultaneously, often in different styles and also taking up painting again.

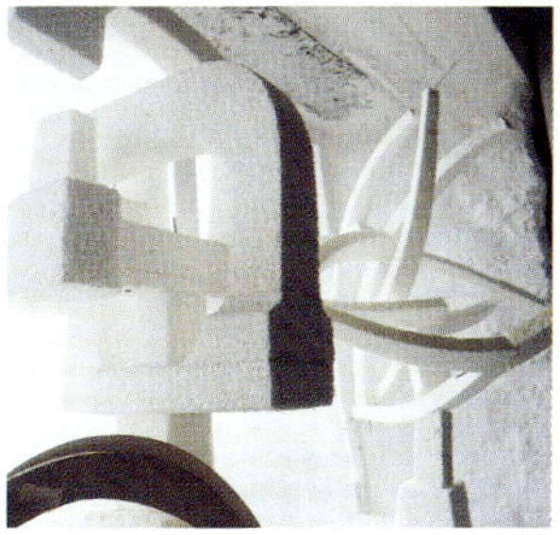

ANTON NICKSON

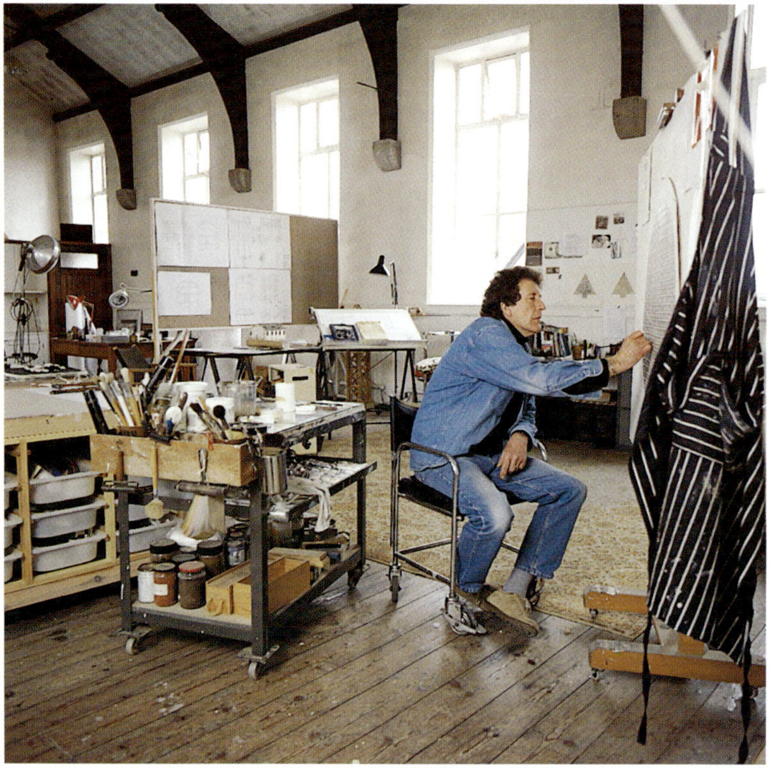

Anton Nickson was born in Brighton. As a child he travelled with his parents living in Malaysia and visiting West Africa and India. He studied painting and sculpture at St Martin's School of Art. In 1967, whilst a student, his work was selected for the 'Young Contemporaries at the Tate'. He has since exhibited widely in London and the South West. He has worked as a freelance architectural designer in London, Paris and Italy and taught printmaking at Croydon College before moving to Cornwall in 1994. He is the current Chairman of the Newlyn Society of Artists.

Coming Home Early
2001
680 x 570mm
mixed media

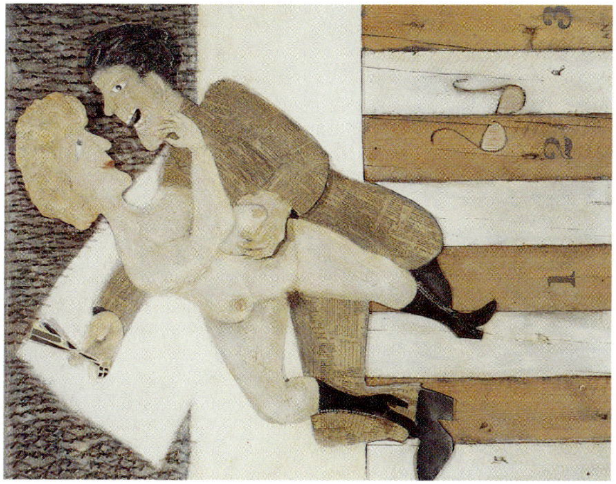

I moved to St Ives following the chance discovery of a large Methodist Sunday School that, after conversion has provided me with near-ideal living and working space. At first the overwhelming local beach culture exerted a strong influence on my work. I have since returned to my continuing concerns with sexuality, mortality and the reinterpretation of historical and literary concepts.

I construct my work mainly from ephemera, which I'm constantly searching out and collecting. Much of this material forms the starting point for an idea that often develops into an abbreviation for something more complex and thought provoking. I like to place these constructions within boxes. I think that a work should include more experience than a simply intended statement. I enjoy living and working on the edge - where the land falls to the ocean.

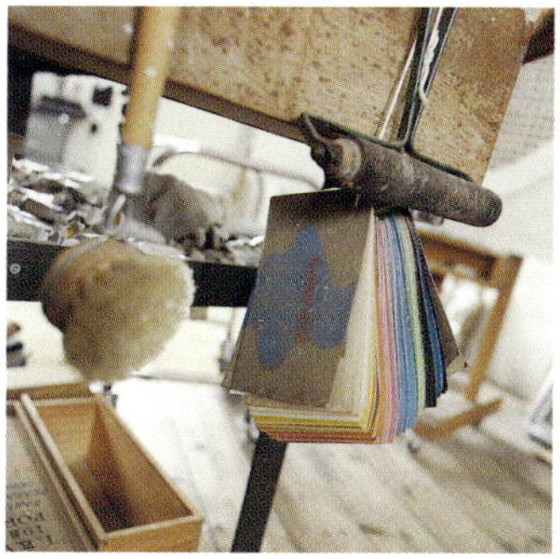

BREON O'CASEY

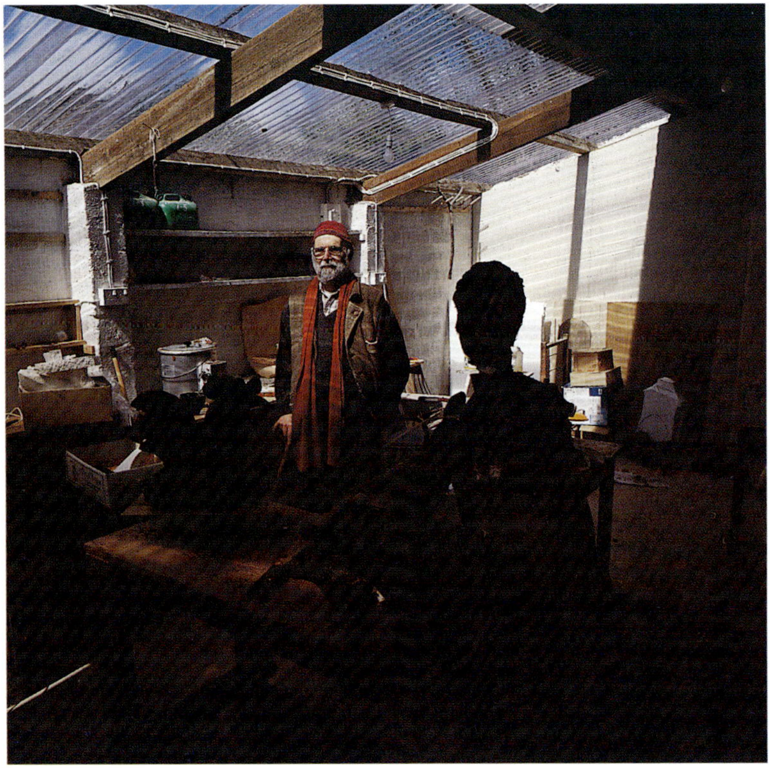

Primarily a painter, Breon O'Casey is also well-known for jewellery, sculpture, printmaking and weaving. His jewellery can be seen in the V&A Museum. Born in London in 1928 he studied painting at the Anglo-French Art Centre in London. He came to St Ives in the late 1950s and worked as an assistant first to Denis Mitchell and later to Barbara Hepworth. He lives and works at Paul near Mousehole.

Cup Bird
2000
height 360mm
bronze

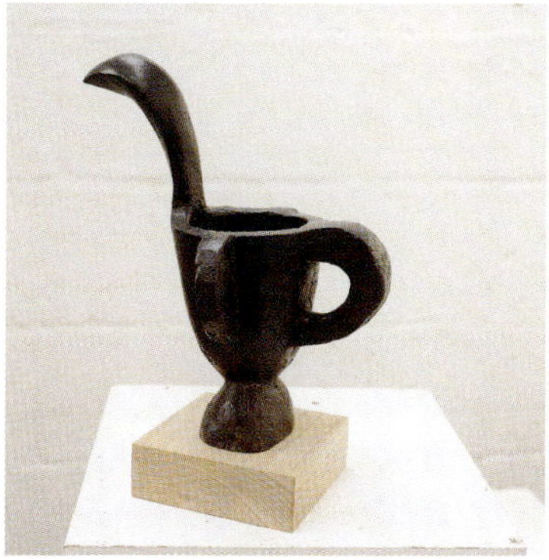

In the 50s, if you were a 'modern artist', you were quite lonely as there was a lot of antipathy towards it, so I decided to move to St Ives because there were are lot of artists there. Painting is my first love but I started making jewellery to earn a living. It was very pleasant but I didn't want to devote all my time to it and finally gave it up when I was seventy.

From working with Denis Mitchell, I learnt to enjoy the tedium of work. He was an extremely, kind and gentle man. Barbara Hepworth was very difficult to work for but she was the first professional artist I knew and there was a big difference between a professional artist and a struggling artist. Barbara used to say to me, 'Even if you don't do anything, you should go into the studio every day' and that has been good advice: to keep the momentum going is very important. I liked the rhythms of sculpture but for me it came later, I did try to sculpt while working with Denis and Barbara, but I could never see in three dimensions.

The past interests me: the shock of the old. I find any shocks I get now are from old things, not from new things. I would still create things if no one was to ever see them or if no one liked them. Success hasn't been important to me, financially it has but it doesn't particularly please me when people say they like my work, which gives me the benefit of not giving a damn if no one does likes it, like the Miller of Dee.

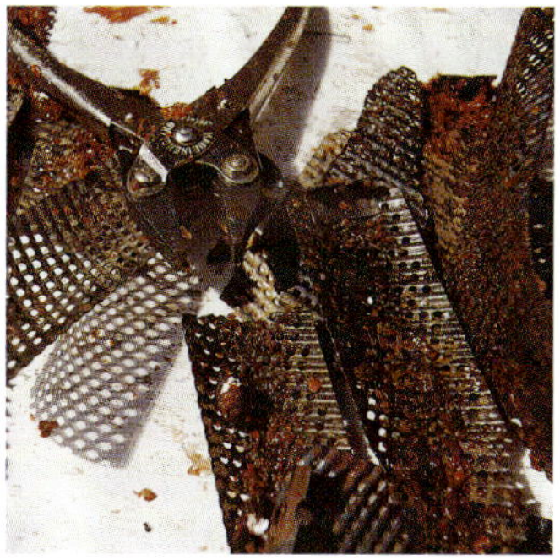

BIDDY PICARD

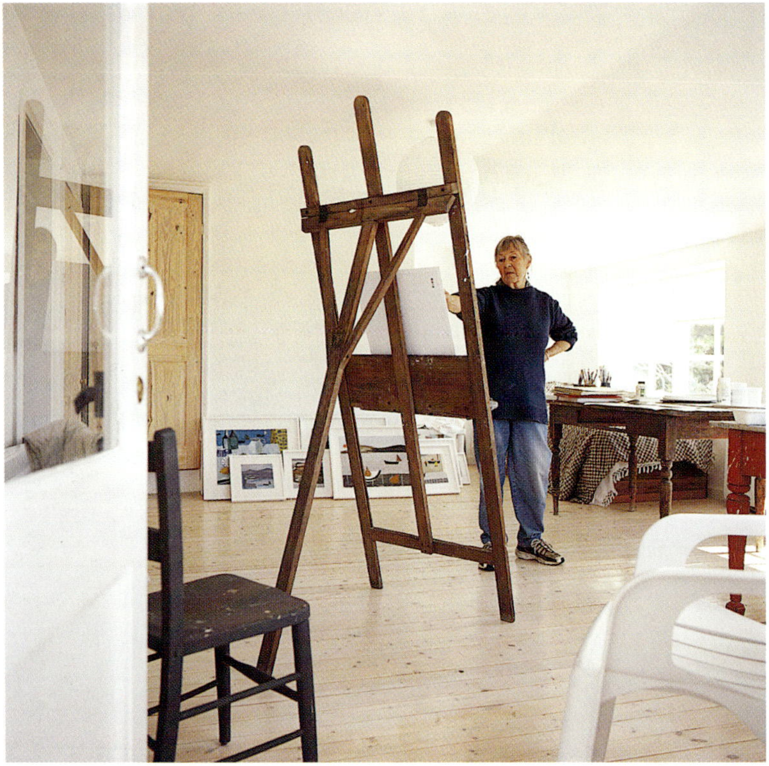

Derbyshire born, Biddy Picard studied at Chesterfield School of Art and the Slade. She then taught at Badmington School, Bristol before settling in Penwith in 1949. She lives and works at Paul near Mousehole.

What the Storm Left
2001
500 x 600mm
acrylic on canvas
board

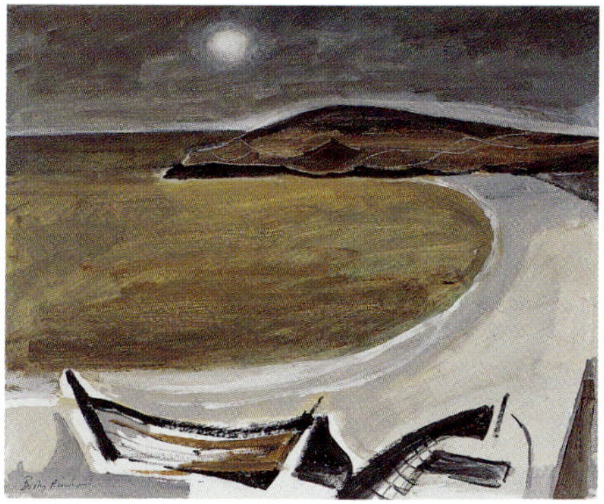

During the war I met and married one of a group of conscientious objectors seeking a simple, back to nature lifestyle. Joining the group in North Wales, I later walked down the Welsh coast to Milford Haven and, after a chance sea passage in a French crabber, arrived in Newlyn. With its brilliant light, blue seas and skies and brightly painted local and French fishing boats, West Cornwall seemed indeed a 'foreign land' - a far cry from the dark mountains and valleys of North Wales.

So began a new life in Cornwall, first at Lamorna living with my family in a gypsy caravan, cooking on campfires, washing in the stream and often sleeping under the stars. Later in Mousehole, together with my husband Bill, we established the Mousehole Pottery and Craftshop, selling both our own work and that of other local potters and craftspeople. I began making stoneware ceramic sculptures and was at the same time, painting and drawing. I exhibited at the Newlyn Society of Artists, becoming a committee member, and also taught for a period at Penzance School of Art.

After a move to the moors near Paul, I established 'Animal Friends', a successful business making stoneware ceramic animals. My own ceramic work also continued to develop, becoming increasingly decorated as time went on. Inevitably this led me once more to my original love, painting on board and canvas, which I now concentrate on exclusively.

For me painting is like music, with its own song to sing - colour and shape creating mood and atmosphere in an attempt to capture the wildness, strength and magic of this fist of land thrust into the sea: Penwith.

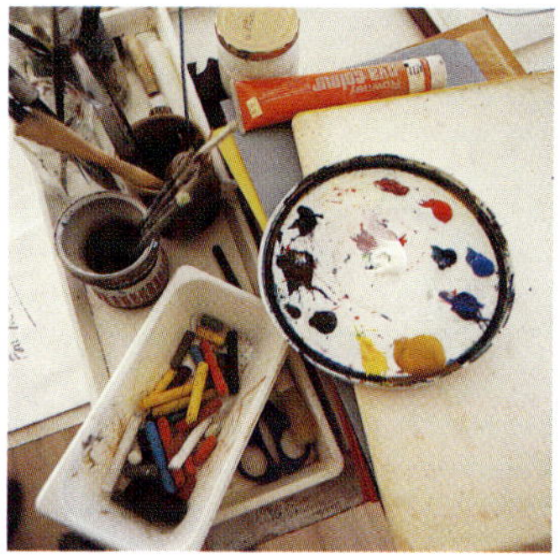

NEIL PINKETT

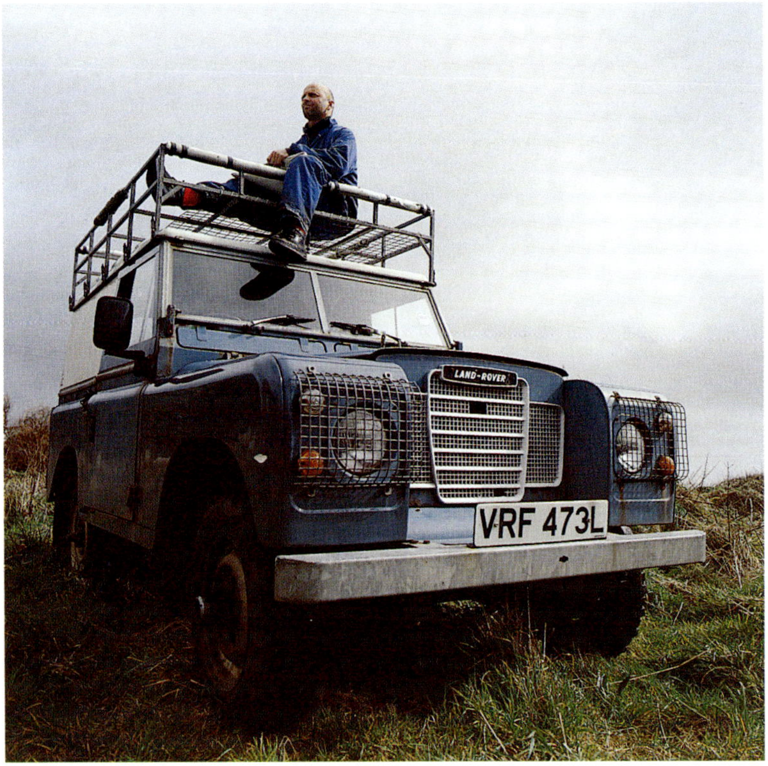

Neil Pinkett was born in St Just. He has realised a childhood ambition to be a painter via a design and illustration background. He has a special affinity with the landscape of the Penwith peninsula where he grew up and is now part of the artistic community. He works from his studio on the moors close to Penzance.

Marazion Beach
2000
460 x 510mm
oil on board

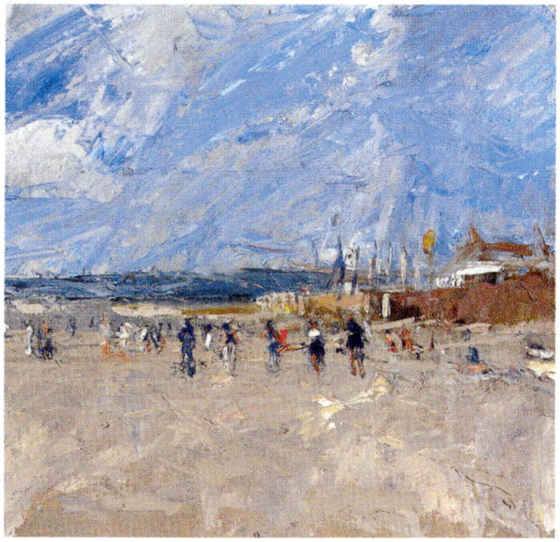

I spend a lot of time observing the ever-changing climatic conditions that make for such dramatic landscape. I walk the beaches and cliffs daily, sketching and painting 'en plein air'.

My paintings are really studio-based. Starting from a drawing on the canvas I lay down a foundation, then work very quickly and energetically for hours or days. I have found working with oil a great challenge and joy, through which I hope to convey my passion for this environment of raging seas and untamed moors.

Often the initial subject matter is a starting point only, as the painting takes on a life of its own. I am constantly reassessing my relationship with this landscape that I feel I know so intimately.

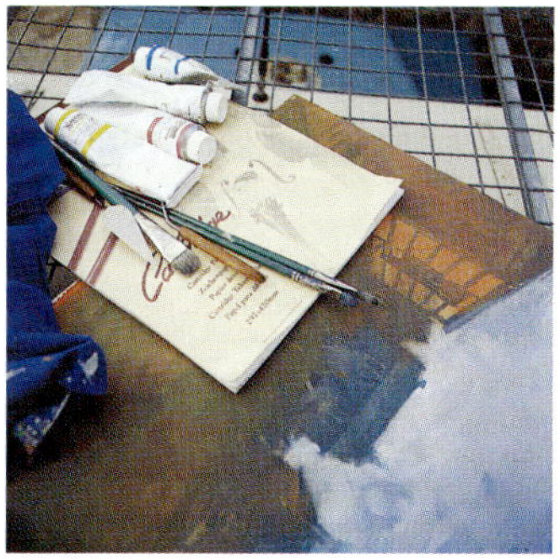

SIMON POOLEY

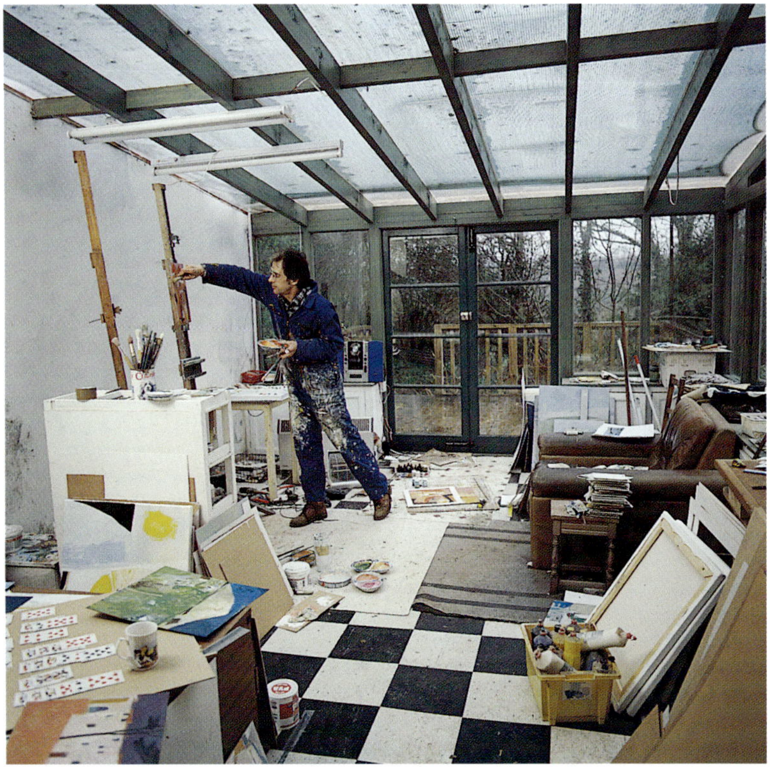

Simon Pooley, born in Cheshire in 1955, trained as an architect in London and spent the following twelve years practising architecture in Sheffield. He moved to St Buryan in 1992 and has since painted full-time.

Embarkation
915 x 760mm
oil on board

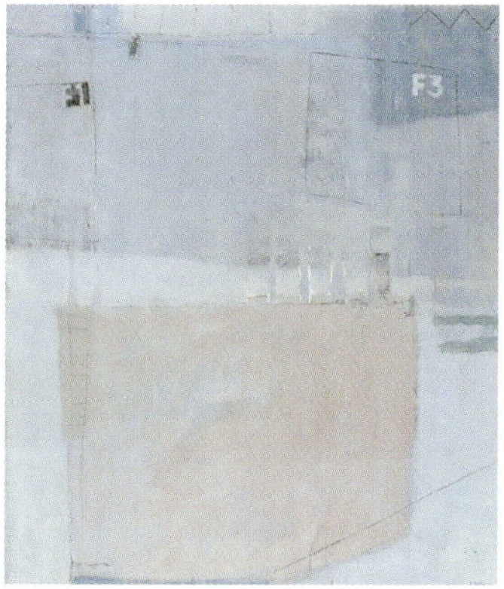

I entertain the conceit that you can't get a much better education than one in architecture. There is nothing like the discipline of learning how to design buildings for honing your creative thought processes. It nurtures creative expression but I've found painting to be more liberating. I enjoyed architecture but thought I ought to be doing what I was best at and didn't know how good a painter I could be and wanted to find out.

I draw all the time; I've always got a sketchbook in my pocket and I'm used to having a pencil in my hand - it's more natural than using a knife or fork. In the studio drawing reinforces my memory, I don't think you've really seen something until you've drawn it. It's logged in and is available for recollection at any time. Memory edits things, instead of remembering all the leaves on the trees and all the cattle in the fields you only remember what is important to you at the time. Sometimes it's reduced to an archetype. If I'm painting a landscape, it's not the place I want to paint but my response to that place. I paint because I've seen something and want to experience it again, albeit in a different way.

Usually when I wake up I can hardly wait to finish breakfast and get to the studio. Sometimes high expectations kill my creativity, if I've painted well the week before I have to forget this and get on with it. I only have one ambition and that is to become better. I'm never completely happy with what I've done but if at the end of a year I think I'm a better painter than I was at the beginning, then I'm happy.

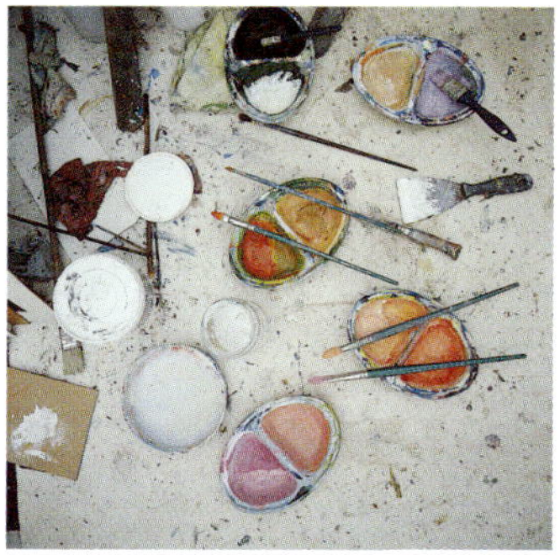

ROY RAY

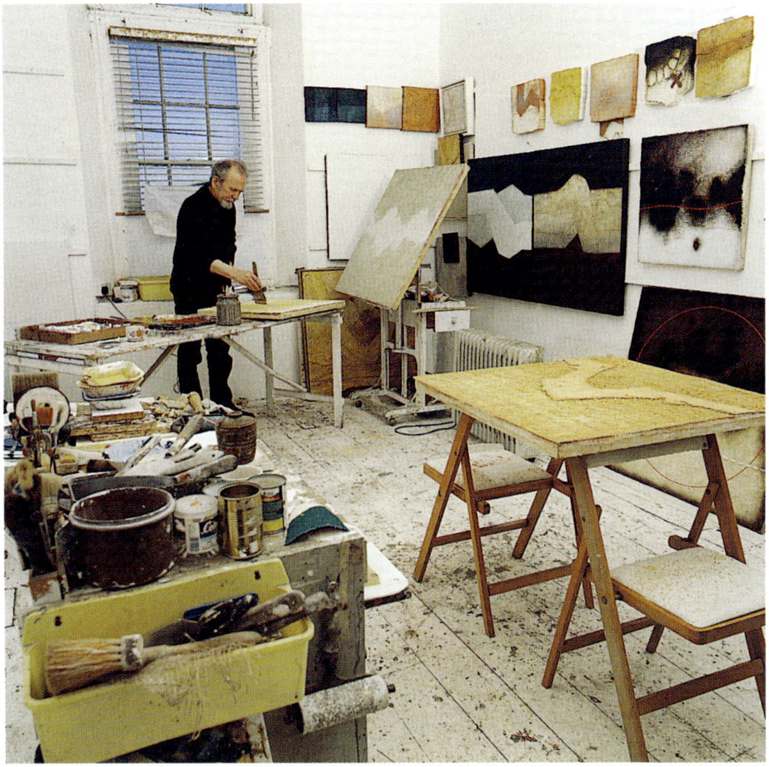

Roy Ray is well known for his connection with the St Ives School of Painting, of which he was principal for 24 years. Born in 1936 in Middlesex, he came to live in St Ives in 1974.

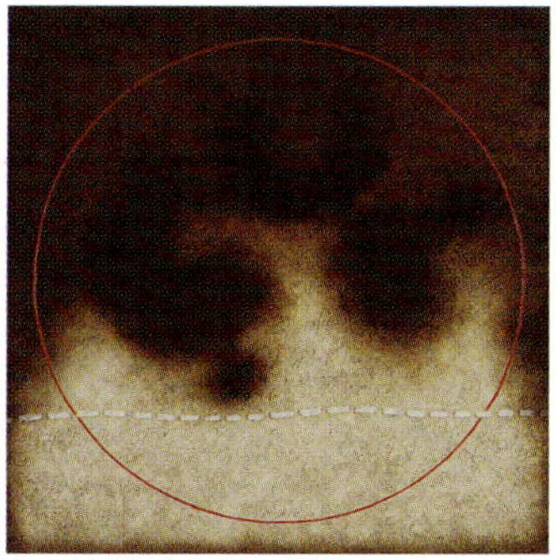

Solar Red
2001
315 x 315mm
oil on mixed
media

I have always enjoyed drawing and can remember as a small child adding drawings to my mother's letters to my father during the war and later doing well at school in art - I particularly liked drawing maps. However, I was in my late twenties, by then married with two children, before I started painting regularly. For many years I painted at weekends only and attended evening classes at Croydon Art College; during this time I began making regular visits to Cornwall.

Following my move to St Ives, I was painting the landscape in a broadly representational style though my instincts were telling me to look beyond its obvious outward appearance. The influence of contemporary painting in St Ives led to the use of collage in my work allowing me to make references to local geology, archaeology, weathered surfaces and the ancient language. But it was a chance flight in a light aircraft from St Just in 1979 that became the pivotal moment in my artistic journey. From 1000 feet I saw below me what I always knew existed: a landscape without space, rendered flat, no horizon, no top or bottom, just texture and colour. For me the dilemma had been resolved by this fusion of seemingly opposing artistic forces - realism and abstraction.

Now, over twenty years later I am making paintings and objects with a vocabulary of irregular shapes, textured surfaces, muted colours, fragments of writing and signs none of which are intended to have a specific meaning beyond the energies and emotions of a particular moment. However, these 'spontaneous' works frequently and I suppose, inevitably touch upon some aspects of this rich environment and the journey I have made.

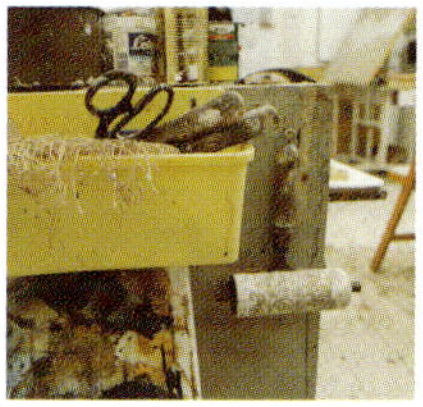

TOM RICKMAN

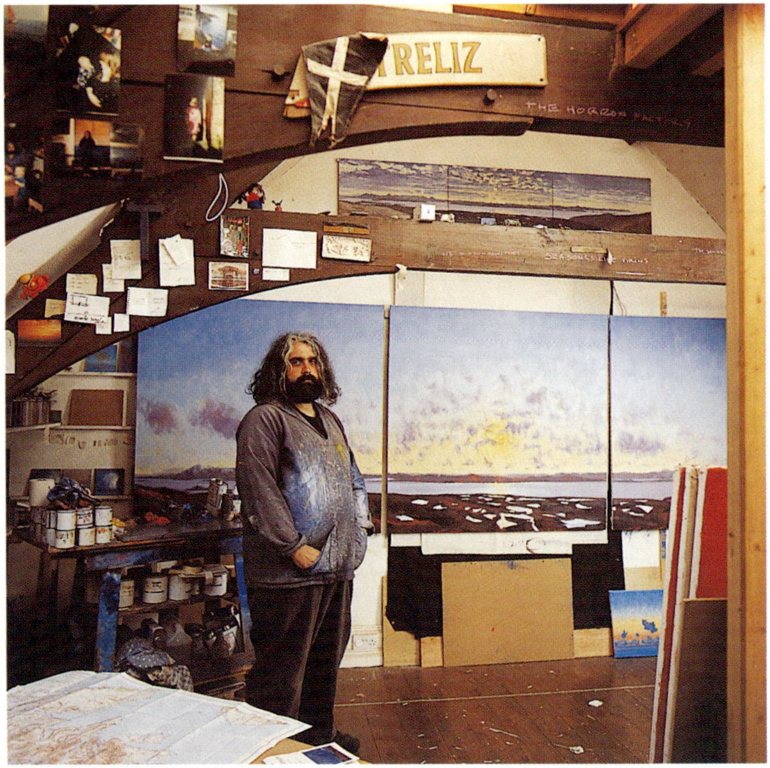

Tom Rickman was born in London in 1960. He studied at Epson College of Art and Design. He moved to West Dorset in 1983 to ‘be amongst the landscape’ and remained there for nine years working from a beach hut. He moved to Penwith in 1993 where he still lives and works.

Wester
315 x 1370mm
oil on canvas
(Steve Tanner)

While I was at college I worked in an abstract manner producing large colour-field paintings involving light and colour which was a response to my experience of the landscape. Working directly and intuitively in this way allowed me to produce work that took qualities of light and atmosphere and enhanced it in a more expressive way. Moving to live in the landscape I was inspired to represent the subject and its romantic possibilities.

I find drawing outside essential, the process giving me the information and images I'll later use. The direct manner of drawing allows me to grasp the essence of the moment leaving a residue or memory I can evolve in the studio. The gap between the experience and the inception of the work can be days, weeks or years so I suppose I have a long thread of ideas about the landscape running through my work. My point of interest is the horizon and can be seen as a metaphor for this longevity. The furthest point as an edge, a place of transition and tension. There seems to be an unbroken continuous, horizontal line that divides my paintings, a compositional no-no but I like this divisional element.

Painting gives me a sense of place and a connection to a moment experienced which I and the viewer can experience and return to. I'm not of the expressionist school; I'm not churning out my raw emotions. The natural world is an incredible array of possibilities and I wish to do some homage to that physical big space. Hopefully within the painting there is more than just a picture of a place but also an element that is to do with paint and expression, that's the me in it I suppose - my creativity.

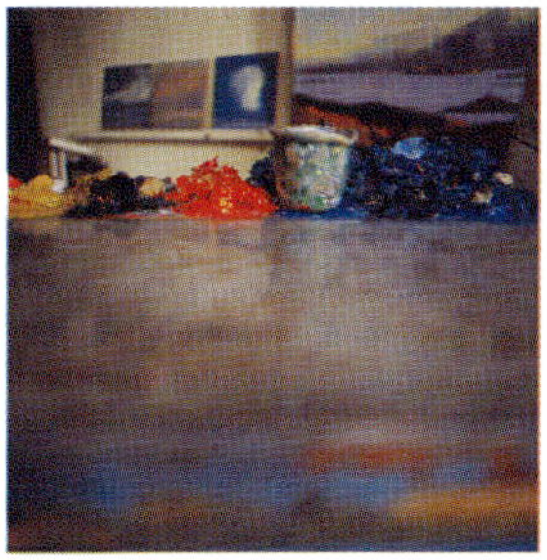

ALEX SMIRNOFF

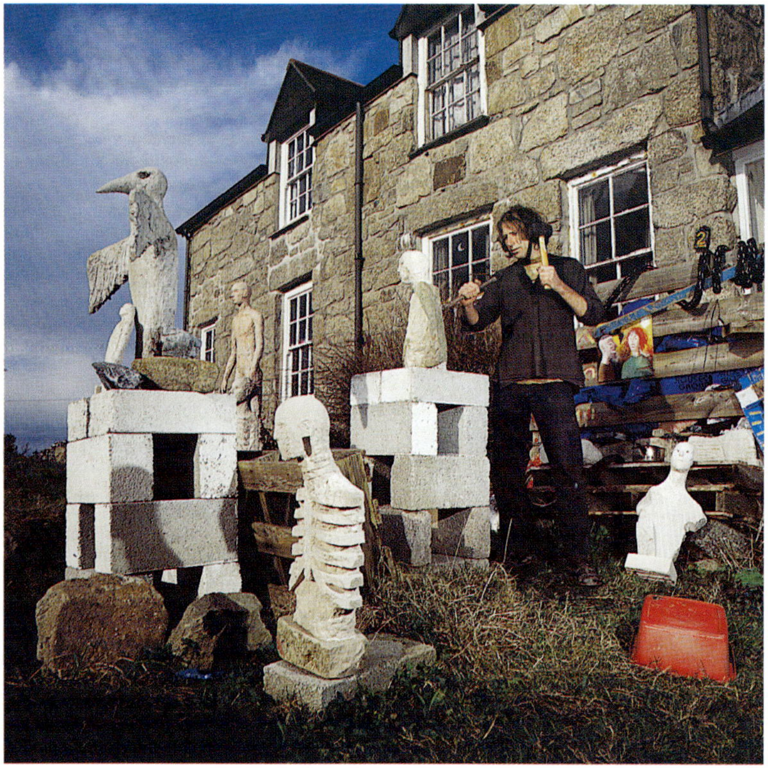

London born, Alex Smirnoff studied graphics at West Sussex College of Design. He worked as an illustrator in London before settling near St Just in 1987. He spends his time sculpting, painting and making music.

Untitled
2001
height 920mm
hamhill stone

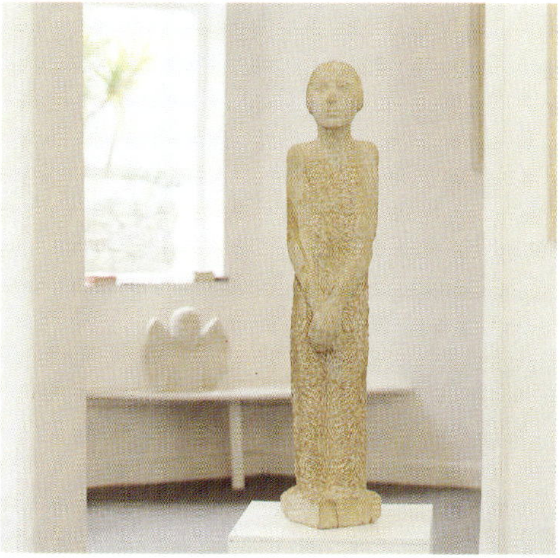

When I gave up illustrating to become a painter, my work was based on my frequent trips to Cornwall and the folklore surrounding its ancient sites, so it seemed natural to move here.

I've always been interested in sculpture and attended a carving course at Portland. My work has consisted almost exclusively of sculpture ever since, but in the background painting is always there, I feel that I must paint to prove something to myself. I don't want to get trapped into one way of working. I'm just whatever I am - an artist. If you are creative why not make music, paint, sculpt, make an installation, whatever it takes to express what's inside you.

My work is about connecting with how I feel inside. Sometimes what I'm doing can feel wrong and then suddenly I create a mark or remove a piece of stone and it feels right, I can't intellectualise why, it's just a connection. My subject matter comes from the imagination and my tendency is to shut the door and live in my own private world but it's great being where there are so many other creative people.

I'm an artist because it gives pleasure and some meaning to my existence but I also get enjoyment from showing my work. I am lucky that some people connect with what I'm doing and feel touched by it. Sometimes people say that my work can be strange and scary and I enjoy these comments just as much, because if I can get a reaction either way, then that's great.

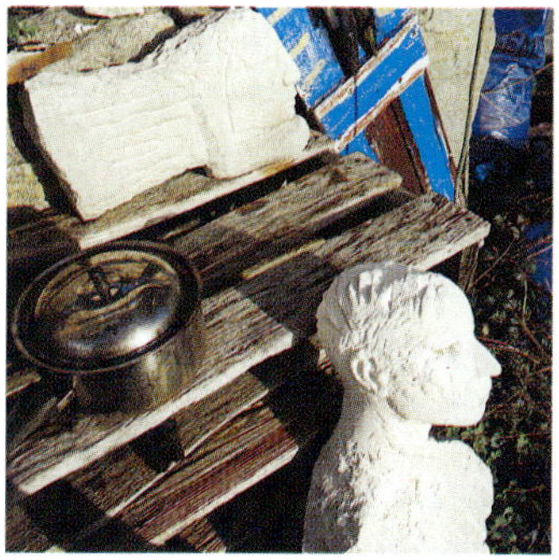

MARY STORK

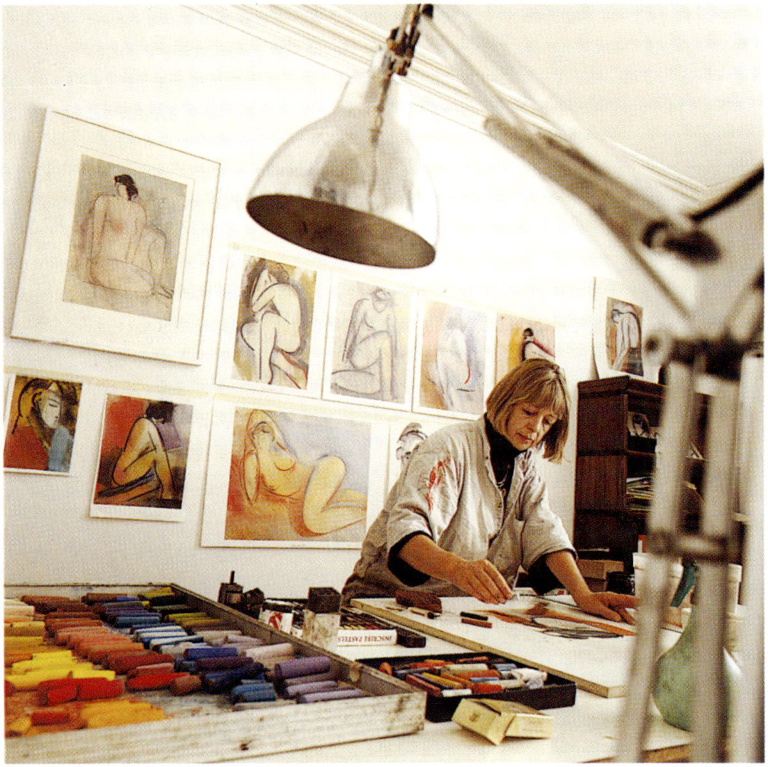

Mary Stork was born in Portsmouth. She studied at the West of England College of Art and the Slade where she won major awards and toured with the Arts Council. Settling in St Just in the early 1960s, she now lives in Penzance. She is a member of the Penwith Society of Arts and Newlyn Society of Artists.

Destiny
14.4.01
710 x 505mm
mixed media
(Dom Mansbridge)

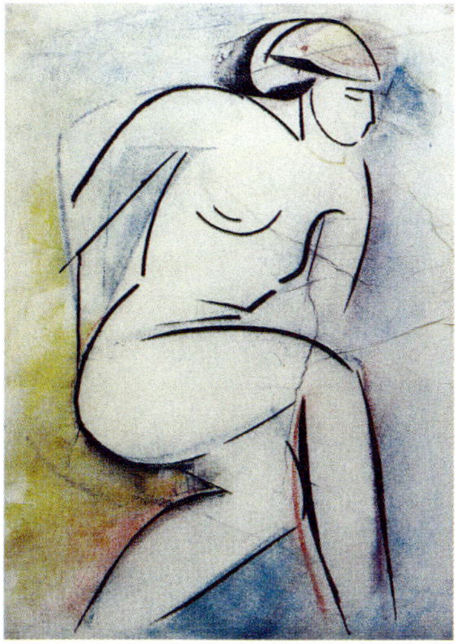

My main tutor at the West of England College of Art was Paul Feiler and he encouraged me to visit Cornwall in the late 1950s when the St Ives School was flourishing. I moved to St Just in 1960 with my first husband Jeremy Le Grice. Karl Weschke who also lived in the area, had an enormous influence on me and then the arrival of the Hiltons in 1966 gave me further encouragement. I gave up painting full time for eighteen years when I remarried and brought up my family in Porthleven. On returning to West Penwith in 1982, I restarted painting professionally and had absorbed so much that I was overflowing with inspiration.

My influence comes from all different cultures and every artist at some time has affected my work. I was fortunate to be taught by EH Gombrich at the Slade along with Frank Auerbach and Keith Vaughan. Ultimately I'm a Picasso fan who I think was very diverse and covered every spectrum of art.

I am a figure painter portraying emotions of women; my models provide me with energy, information and discipline. Colour is not necessarily what I'm seeing visually but is connected to an emotional feeling in a very subtle way. Every line is a commitment and is subsequently supported by another line and finally creates balance and rhythm. Painting is all about energy, you can grab hold of it and put it instantly into ones work. I'm always looking for my own perfection and risk losing a picture to take it that one step further.

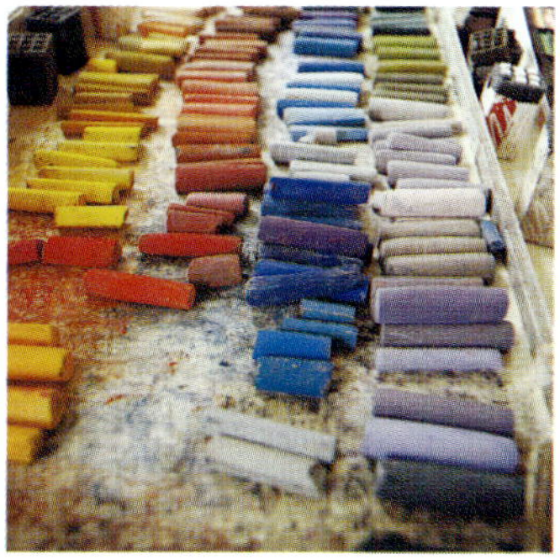

MAURICE SUMRAY

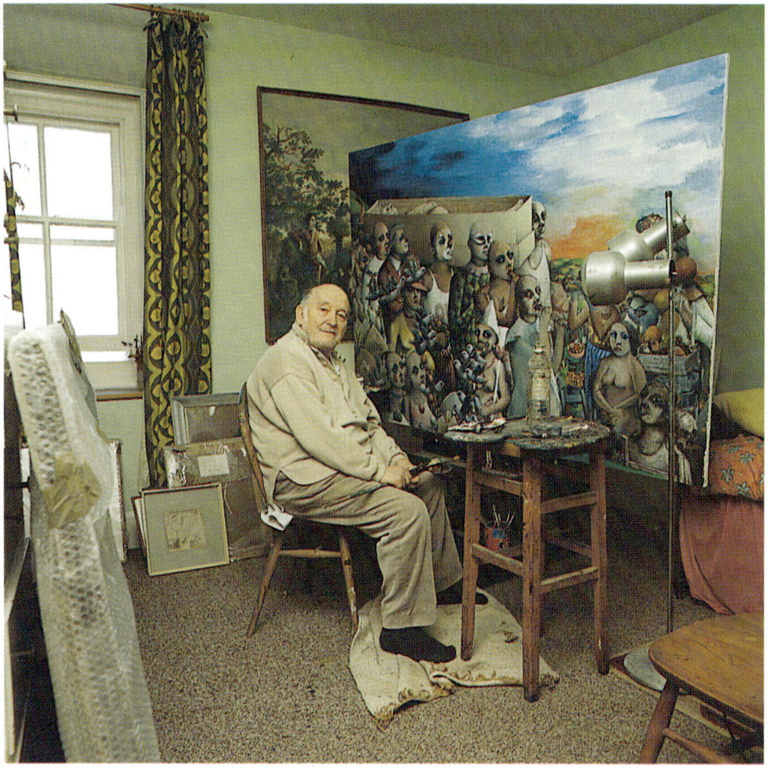

London born, Maurice Sumray has a background in engraving. In 1949, at the age of 29 he won a scholarship to Goldsmith's College. The British Museum purchased two of his works and he has exhibited in the Chicago International Exposition, USA. He moved to St Ives in 1968.

The Crowning of Creir
1993
1850 x 1240mm
oil on canvas

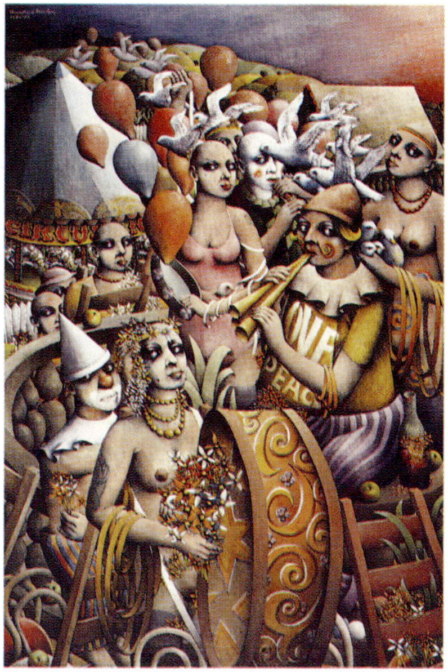

I have painted since the age of seven or eight but my father wanted me to take up a profession so I became an engraver. I decided to go to Goldsmith's and had my very first major exhibition in London the month I started there. The paintings I did then were much better than the work I became known for. Why my work changed I've no idea but I believe I was a better painter then. I think I became influenced by my earlier engraving, which was very linear. I moved to Cornwall reluctantly because my dear wife wanted to for some romantic idea. It was nothing to do with art and I didn't paint for the first two or three years that we were here. I still don't like St Ives, it's just a seaside resort. I've always been more concerned with the European scene.

I haven't painted much over the last eighteen months because I'm ill. I have a big painting on the easel and I keep saying to myself I've got to finish it even if it's the last one I ever do, but I'm a bit disenchanted with painting and the significance of painting. My work is the type you either love or hate and the people who love them must see their sensuous side. Painting is a passion but for me there are other passions, one minute you love it, the next you hate it. I'd sooner play a game of poker.

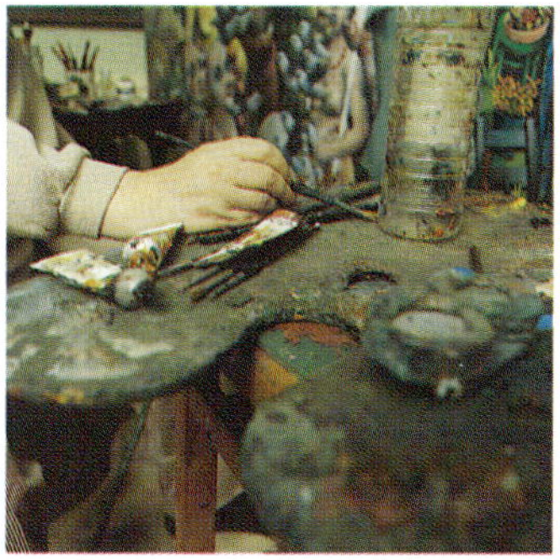

MICHAEL UPTON

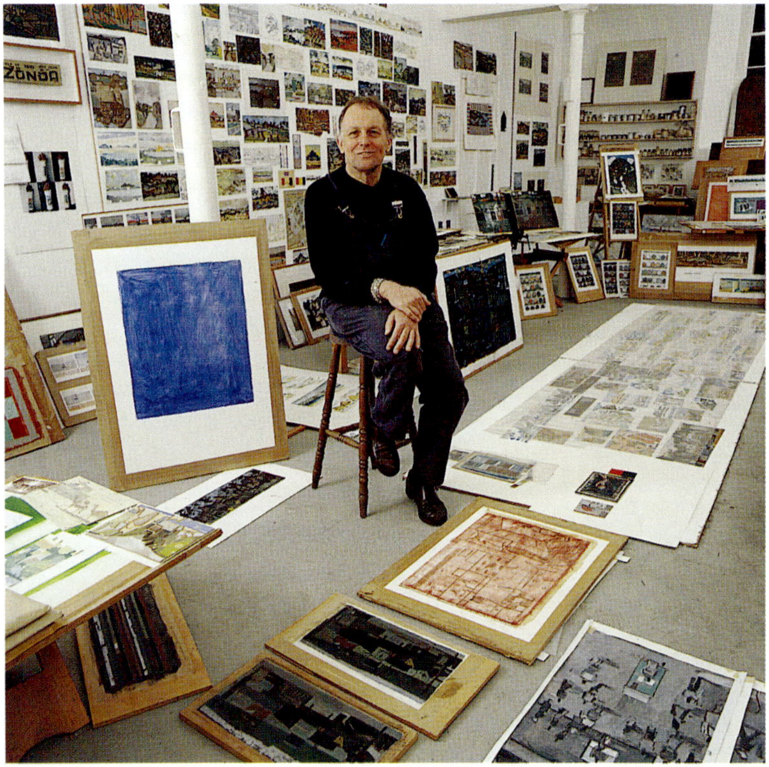

Michael Upton was born in Birmingham in 1938. He studied at Birmingham College of Art and the Royal Academy where he is now a Senior Lecturer in painting. He has received many awards including a Rome Scholarship to Italy in 1962, the South West Arts Major Award in 1981 and the Singer and Friedlander Prize (Sunday Times) in 1993. He lives and works in Mousehole.

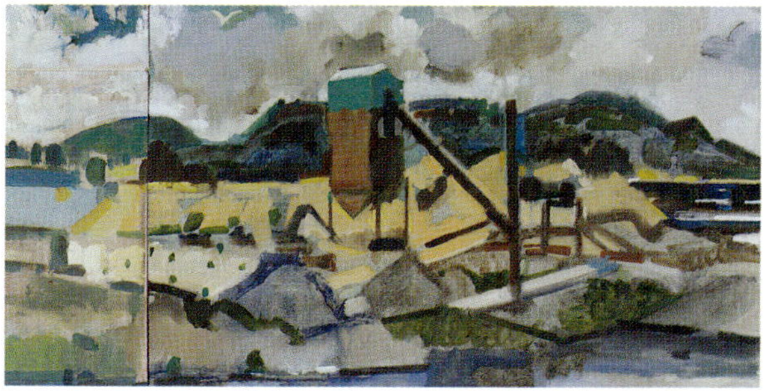

Sandpit
2000
280 x 530mm
oil on board

I was interested in the history of art in West Penwith when I moved to the chapel in Mousehole in 1996. In London I worked on both installations (with Peter Lloyd Jones) and small scale paintings of city matters such as cafes, tabletops and tube stations. Upon moving to Cornwall my palette became more varied, the subject matter changed and the scale of work became larger. The work involves studio-based compositions and certain works based on landscape, with the repetition of images. The recent paintings combine figuration, abstraction and text and a sense of place is always important in all work.

At the moment I am teaching part time at the Royal Academy Schools and the Royal College but I'm there less now than I used to be as I'm spending more time painting in Cornwall and travelling. Damien Hurst was one of my students as was Tracey Emin and she's now a great friend of mine.

I am interested and involved in contemporary painting and my particular involvement is with the concepts of idea based painting. I don't care for art that's not about processes or thinking before it is made.

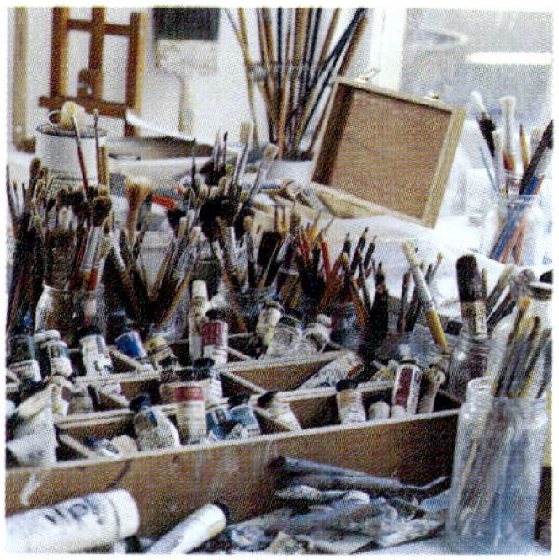

GILL WATKISS

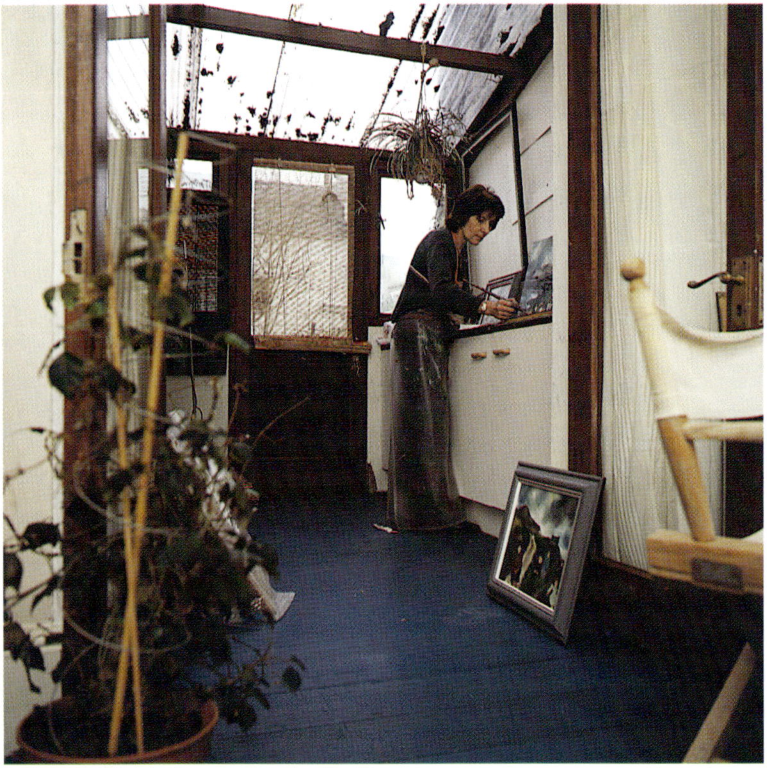

London born, Gill Watkiss studied at the Walthamstow School of Art before coming to live in Newlyn in 1959. She then moved to St Just, where she stayed for eight years. She now lives and works in Penzance.

The Parade's Gone By - a Darker Day Than Usual
2000
635 x 990mm
oil on board

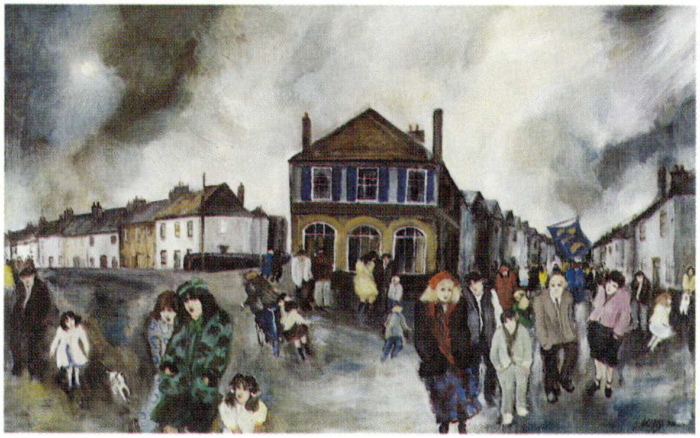

When I moved to Cornwall from London it took ages for me to establish my own identity as a painter. The countryside presented such a different space that I couldn't adapt my former painting approach to the experiences of it. I didn't know what to paint and was very frustrated. When we moved to St Just I remember visiting the playing field and watching children playing in the wind blown park under a threatening sky, wispy creatures blown around the landscape. I rushed home, cleared the breakfast things aside and tried to capture what I had seen and been so moved by. It was the stepping stone that helped me connect with the visual ideas from my beginnings as a painter.

I paint the landscape first then feel the people into it like shadows, gradually working the two together. I'm interested in the emotional impact a landscape has on people, how it fashions them physically. It doesn't matter if details differ; I'm not presenting a photographic record but an atmospheric impression.

My idea of a good day is getting up and going straight into the studio. I sometimes consider what life would have been like if I hadn't wanted to paint. I never thought when I began that it would be this engulfing obsession that invades my thoughts even in the middle of the night. I'm always thinking of the next painting and work as if I'm writing my diary. I don't want to do anything else but I'm aware that obsessions can be enclosing to the extent that you have nothing of interest to say and I'm always looking to avoid this.

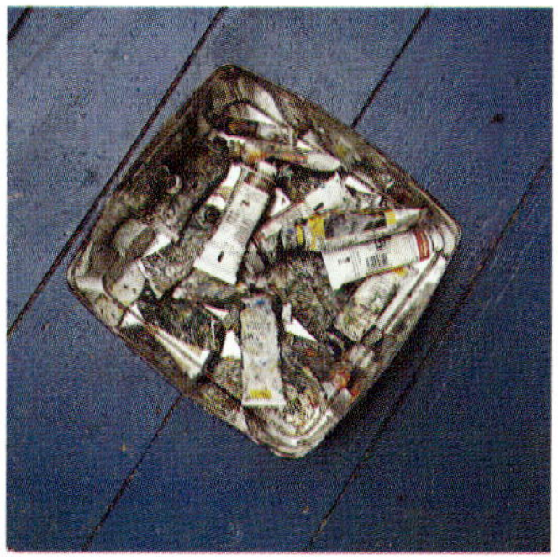

PARTOU ZIA

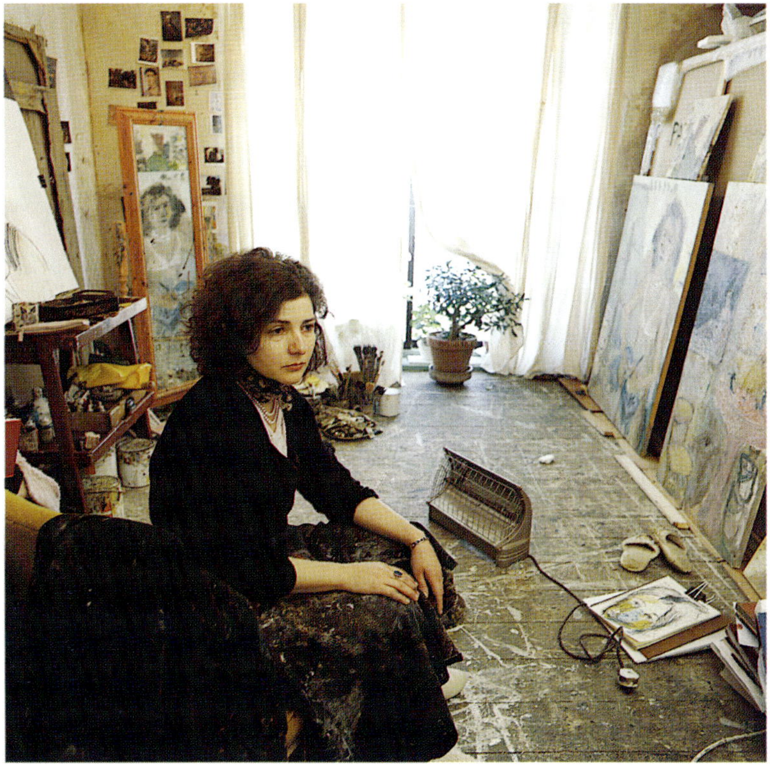

Born in Tehran in 1958, Partou Zia moved to London when she was eleven. She studied at Warwick University and the Slade School of Art, moving to Newlyn in 1993 where she lives and works.

Green Stairs
2001
206 x 99mm
oil on canvas

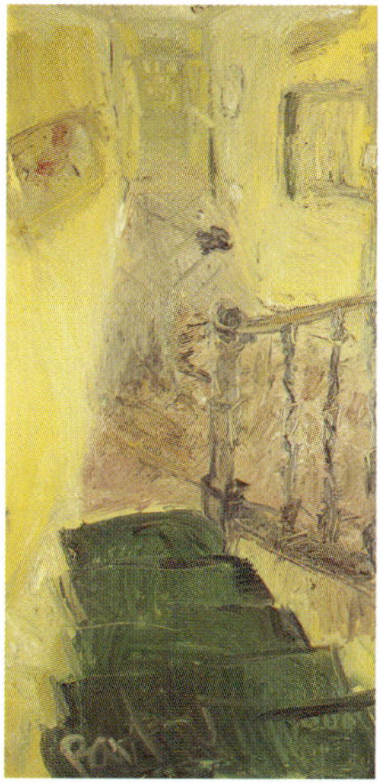

painting from myself - exploring self-portraiture as the presence of a body (myself) observed in the mirror within the domestic place I inhabit. My interest is not subject matter per se, but through paint that allows presence to be given form.

The impulse behind my painting is experience: by this I mean being mindful of sensation from both within myself and my immediate environment. I draw that which interests me, often ordinary objects or aspects of an interior. The way light catches a corner or a chair becomes, through involvement with paint, a subject in itself. This intimacy with my own vernacular space extends to the ecclesiastic interior of St Peter's, Newlyn. Through drawing I sense the intrinsic shape of things as delineated by light. My need is to find a spiritual possibility. Parallel with the interiors I am engaged in

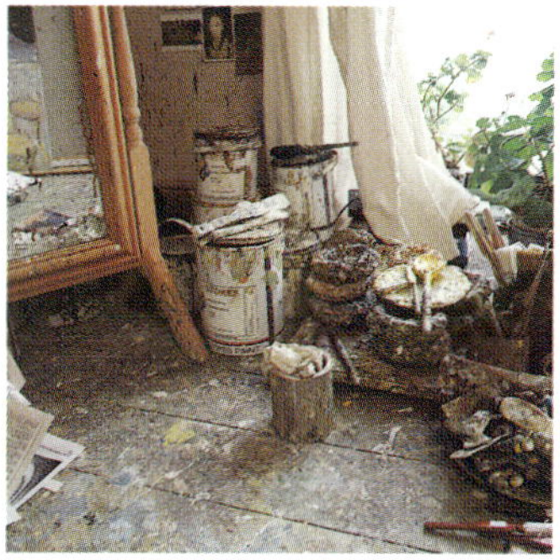

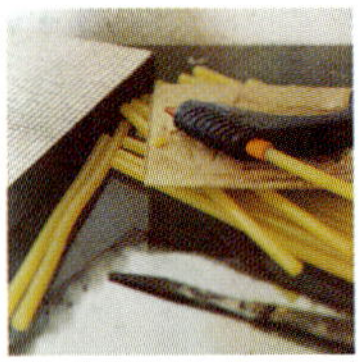